MW00510656

KYLE O'REILLY

Kyle O'reilly

Copyright © 2020 by John Green. All rights reserved.

No part of this publication may be reproduced, stored in a retrieval system, or transmitted in any form or by any means, digital, electronic, mechanical, photocopying, recording, or otherwise, or conveyed via the Internet or a website without prior written permission of the publisher, except in the case of brief quotations embodied in critical articles and reviews.

ISBN: 978-1-7363082-3-3 (paperback)
         978-1-7363082-4-0 (ebook)

Printed in the United States of America

KYLE O'REILLY

JOHN GREEN

TABLE OF CONTENTS

CHAPTER 1

Kyle O'Reilly was born to Barnabas and Catherine O'Reilly, immigrants from Dublin, Ireland. Barnabas and Katie, as Barnabas called her, had moved to America landing in New York, not finding any work; on hearing of work in Virginia in the mines, they moved to Virginia and went to work at a coal mine, a year later, Kyle was born the first of seven children. They had five boys and two girls.

For two years they lived in a boarding home, then they moved into a house of their own, two years later close to a horse ranch, it was also near the mine, Katie was able to get a job cleaning the houses for some of the ranchers.

As Kyle grew up he began to work cleaning the horse stalls when he was ten years old, at twelve years old he began helping to train horses, he had a natural knack at training horses, Kyle gained a love for horses and a dream started to grow for the Wild West.

A friend had given him a book about a rancher in Texas, and it was about roundups and Indians and it all sounded like great adventure, at twelve years old he started saving his money, he did not want to work in the mines.

Kyle was built a little more like his mother's side of the family, Katie was a hair taller than Barnabas, who was five ten tall, but if he can get under it, it would move.

Kyle was strong, he was not as wide as his dad, though at twelve he was almost as tall as Barnabas, at sixteen he's was six two.

The ranch had thoroughbred race horses, though Kyle had bested the jockeys time he was too big to compete in the big races.

Kyle had a way about getting the best out of a horse, he could feel how they set, he could help or hurt their speed by leaning that way this way, and this would help them The ranch owner was able to see Kyle's talent and used it to help win many races.

Kyle's brother Barnabas was next to him in age, not only did he have his father's name he was built like his father also, he did not like horses as Kyle did and he started working at the mine at fifteen, him and Kyle were eleven months apart, his next brother was named after his grandfather, Katie's dad, Jamison, they call him Jim, he was built more like Kyle, and he was working with horses, the rancher thought perhaps one of them would stay on, he had seen Kyle with a few dime novels of the west and he could see a longing in him, he seem to just love working with the horses plus he loved to help his daughter Nancy with riding, but she was sweet on Jim, but Mike Dorsey, he is the rancher he could see the difference in the liking in Jim was who she preferred, she had also said Kyle had talked about going west someday, Buck hoped he'd be able to teach Jim how to read horses before he did. Jim was doing okay, but had a long way to go to get to be as good as Kyle.

Next family member was Alyssa named after her grandmother, Barnabas mother, she was twelve, next was another brother, Robert named after their grandfather Barnabas's dad, next to Robert was his sister called Sarah, she was named after Katie's mother she was seven and last was Peter. He was named after Peter in the Bible and it looked as though he was named well, he spoke up about everything, and time would only tell he was just six.

There hadn't been any more children after Peter, which was all right with Katie, more would have been fine but seven was enough, she didn't know if she could have kept up with more, if they would have been like Peter the boy wasn't afraid of anything, much, he couldn't walk on water but he tried every mud puddle he came to, because his name came out of the Bible he wanted to know everything else that did also and if he didn't he wanted to know why.

One thing it had done, it had made Barnabas and Katie, learn more about the bible and yes the mines back then were close on Sunday and the whole family went to Church and while Katie was cooking dinner Barnabas set at the table for an hour answering Peter's questions.

Kyle usually went to church from his boss's house; he drove the coach for them. Buck tried to keep him close so people wouldn't try to steal him away, which they tried quite often.

There were other horse breeders and racers around and quite often they offered Kyle a job, but lucky for Mike Dorsey, who everyone called Buck, he is the ranch owner and as good as Kyle was at raising and training horses, Kyle's dream was not raising the best racehorse but, someday riding the plains of Texas, working cattle.

After dinner on Sundays, which he ate with his family, Kyle would get one of Bucks, riding horses that he was training and head for the mountains, at first Buck didn't like the ideal but, it proved beneficial because more and more people were coming to ask about his riding stock, people who Kyle met here and there on the road they'd ask or comment on his horse and Kyle would tell them it wasn't his horse he just trained them for the Dorsey ranch and also after Kyle road them on long rides. They were gentler and a lot smoother to ride, which helped sell them, as Jim got older he'd have Kyle start training him the way he was using which Buck hoped Jim would pick up and learn how to train the horses as he does, Jim was watching Kyle closely and was learning, and one of the things he had to work on was he wasn't as patient as Kyle was.

One of the things Kyle had told him was with horses you had to use a firm hand but, not a cruel one, work with and learn your horse and no whips.

Barnabas worked hard in the mine and he loved his work and he was glad to have the job and he had hoped all of his son's would follow his trade but, you take each person had their own likes and dislikes, his oldest son, he had seen long ago was going a different path not only drawn by a love for horses, he also wanted some adventure when he got older, he understood adventure that was how he got here to Virginia.

His son Barnabas he would follow him to the mines, his son Jamison would be going to the ranch for a love of a different kind, well he understood that to, he dearly loved his Katie, the rest of his children were a bit young to tell, then he thought of Peter, who knew.

He had just got Home when he was thinking about these things and when the thought of Peter he chuckled and Katie heard Barnabas chuckle.

"What are you chuckling about dear," Katie asked.

"I was thinking about how our children are growing and progressing," Barnabas began.

"And you came to Peter," Katie interrupt him.

"Yeah," Barnabas replied.

"By the time he gets to be Kyle's age there shouldn't be too much he doesn't know," Katie suggested.

"He may have to ask a few more people questions besides us," Barnabas replied.

"True," Katie said, "I suppose that being he's Peter he'll still be seeking answers when he's very old," she added.

"Wisdom comes to those who seek it," Barnabas agreed.

"Then Peter should be a wise man's someday," Katie replied.

"I'm wonder how long before Kyle wants to ride off to the West?" Barnabas asked.

"You don't think some pretty lady would change his mind?" Katie quizzed.

"If he finds a lady she better be able to ride and be ready to move to the West," Barnabas sujested

"A mother can always hope," Katie said.

"Yes, but I'm afraid Kyle has got to find out if the frontier in those books he reads are the place for him," Barnabas explained.

"I know and we were no different," Katie replied, "we had to get on a boat and cross the ocean," she added.

"Yes, we did and I'm very glad; but here is more tame compared to the land where Kyle wants to go," Barnabas replied.

Little did his mother and dad know that this very day, Kyle met a woman, a young lady of his age who sparked his interest, Lillie Mcfactrick, She had red hair and hazel eyes, very shapely in her blue plants and yellow blouse.

Kyle happened to be in the right place to his way of thinking when Lillie's horse bolted he came to her rescue.

They had went up the valley floor in between two mountains for about a mile before Kyle overtook her horse, his calm voice calm not only the horse but Lillie as well, he introduced himself, as he walked both horses to cool them down.

"Hello, my name is Kyle O'Reilly." Kyle introduced. "Hello yourself, my name is Lillie Mcfactrick," Lillie replied, "I'm afraid a snake startled my horse, she's usually as calm as can be, thank you," she added.

"They'll do that sometimes," Kyle agreed, "I've had a few bolts away like yours did" he added.

"Do you live around here?" Lillie asked, hoping to get to know this handsome young man better.

"Not too far," Kyle replied, he was in no hurry to leave, he definitely wanted to get to know this young woman, "I train horses for Mike Dorsey's ranch, it's about twenty miles east of here," he added.

"Isn't that near the little settlement of Morgan, there is a mine there also right?" Lillie asked.

"Yes, my dad works at the mind, its name is Ferguson Coal Company," Kyle answered," Mr. Dorsey's ranch is west of town always, then south we call it Dorsey' Valley, it's about 500 acres plus some grassland in the mountain slopes," he added.

"Pop has a few acres up the Valley a few miles we have grass up in the mountain were we keep our stock when the weather permits, we keep the stock down in the Valley in the winter where we keep our hay, we keep the stock up in the mountain, we have a cabin we stayed in during the summer," Lillie explained, "I had two older brothers, one younger, with two younger sisters, my oldest brother spent a lot of time cutting hay in the Valley in the summer," she added.

"I have seven brothers, I mean in our family five boys, and two girls me and my brother Jim work for Mr. Dorsey, my dad and brother Barnabas work for the mine company," Kyle explained, "the rest are too young to get much of a job, at home we have a milk cow, some pigs and some chickens, and we raised some corn and a garden, we don't have much land," he added.

I work in the garden a lot pulling weeds seems every day," Lillie said.

"There's always that to do," Kyle agreed, "well, it looks like your horse is calmed down and I have a long way to go to get home, but before I go I was wondering if I could," Kyle stumbled. "What I mean do you think it'll be all right with your folks if I come calling on you?" He asked.

"I hope so because I want you to come back," Lillie replied.

"Okay," Kyle smiled and said," how do I find your place next time I come up this way, which will be two weeks because next Sunday I'll be going to a race?" He asked.

"You keep going at this Valley, you'll come to where my brothers are stacking hay, near our home, then you go on past our house and you'll see a road that goes to the left up the mountain, you follow that road, following it till you come out in our upper meadow, then you'll see the cabin," Lillie answered.

"I don't want to but I have to go, it was very nice to meet you Lillie and I'll look forward to the next time," Kyle managed to say, he was very excited by this girl.

"Me too, that is, I'm sorry you have to go, good bye," Lillie said.

Kyle, wave and started back to the ranch, he'd look back a few times and Lillie was still sitting and watching him go. She had never had a boy stir her this way, she wanted to run away with him, but she finally; after one last wave turned her horse and headed home.

The first tree she came to her dad was setting behind on his horse, "who is that?" William Mcfactrick asked.

"The man I'm going to marry,"Lillie replied.

"Oh, now you sound just like your mother did the day we met," her dad said.

"I am my mother's daughter." Lillie replied.

"Full of fire just like her," her dad added.

"At least he asked directions to the house to ask permission to call on me," Lillie informed him.

"Oh, he did; did he, I might be liking this boy a little better than," her dad said, "we'll see," he commented. Her dad was typical of the day protective of the daughter, couldn't let just any boy trying anything improper.

"How did you happen to meet this youngster that you're so already to marry?" Her dad asked.

"Polly was spooked by a snake and he happened to be close by and caught Polly and calmed her down," Lillie replied.

"I see," William said, thinking now I know my daughter and no snake is going to cause her to lose control of Polly,

"I guess you seeing this young feller caused you to forgot how to handle Polly," he added.

"Maybe," Lillie answered, "don't you go telling him Pa," she added.

William laughed, "Polly scared of the snake, how did you get her to run?" He asked. "She'll run when I tell her to." Lillie replied.

"We better be getting home, mother will be putting supper on the table by the time we get there." William said.

"Okay Pa," Lillie replied, but her thoughts were on Kyle, a handsome, strong, young man who saved her from a runaway horse, if her dad didn't let the cat out of the bag, if it had been her brother Bo, he couldn't keep a secret, Richard would. Bo was short for Beauregard; Richard when he was younger couldn't say Beauregard, so their mother told him just to call him Bo, so they did, her mother had named him after her granddad, there mother had joked that they had been more careful with names after Beauregard, so it would be easier for everyone to say and she had named their little brother Ben and their two sisters Lucy and Lou, and there may be one on the way but no name had been suggested yet.

Her mind straying to Kyle, how tall he was and handsome and easy to talk to, she was riding by their turn off when she heard her dad chuckling, she looked up and saw what she'd done, she turned Polly toward the road.

"You seem to have your mind elsewhere," her dad teased.

"Maybe a little," Lillie replied.

"I remember the first time I saw your ma, we met in town walking toward each other, I walked into a pole looking at her," Williams "said.

"What did mom do?" Lilly asked.

"She came over and asked if I was hurt, all concerned, only thing hurt on me was my pride," William answered. "She didn't say it that she was kind of interested in a boy who'd walk into a pole looking at her, although years later she did tell me that had drawn her to me," he added.

"I must have gotten my daydreaming habits from you," Lilly stated.

"Likely so," William agreed, "after I met your mother I couldn't get her out of my mind, I told her she'd have to marry me so I can get that settled in my mind and get my mind back on my work before I got hurt, and she said yes and that I'd been on her mind from time to time, that and she didn't want me to run into any more poles and get hurt," he added, they talked more about Lillie's mother and dads early marriage as they made their way to the cabin in the meadow.

Kyle was practically floating in the saddle on his way back to the Dorsey Ranch, he kept smiling as thoughts of Lillie came into his head, the wild west he'd been reading about didn't come into his mind, it was full of thoughts of the beautiful damsel he had rescued, and what a beautiful woman, it didn't come into his mind she was a girl just sixteen, she looked well filled out where women are supposed to be and girls aren't.

And she said it would be all right if he asked her dad if he could come calling, and she wanted him to, and that she would be impatiently waiting for two weeks to go by.

He has seen lots of pretty women but, none of them had moved him away from his dream like Lillie had. Of course a rose in the wilderness is beautiful and this one has flaming hair.

It was late by the time Kyle returned to the Dorsey Ranch, Buck was a little concerned but not overly, Kyle had been late a time or two; he noticed a smile on Kyle's face right off, though Kyle smiled a lot he was a very serious young man, and not only was he smiling from ear to ear, he was distracted.

"What's her name?" Buck asked, this question caught Kyle off guard.

"What do you mean?" Kyle replied.

"The girl who put that smile on your face and the look in your eye as though you were still looking at their," Buck answered.

"OH "I gave myself away" Kyle began, Lillie McFactrick," he added.

"McFactrick," Buck quizzed, "I know a McFactrick; William has a wife with flaming red hair and what a smile, anyway, I bought a stud off him, that's where Max came from," he explained.

"I'd say Lillie takes after her mother, I'd say she has red hair, a beautiful smile and very shapely for her age," Kyle described.

"I bet that's Williams, daughter," Buck replied, "How did you happen to meet?" He asked.

"I was riding west and cut off up a narrow valley and her horse spooked and started to race up the Valley, so I went after her and caught her horse and walked along with her for a while," Kyle answered.

"I see," Buck replied, "what spooked it?" He asked.

"A snake," Kyle answered, "now that I think about it, she didn't seem afraid, though she wasn't hanging on to the horn, the horse either for that matter," he added.

"Perhaps she wanted to get your attention," Buck suggested.

"Yeah," Kyle replied, "she didn't have to do anything, I was already looking at her," he added.

"Take my advice and keep your thoughts about her horse spooking and her losing control between you and me and don't say anything to anyone else about your suspicions, if you were to confront her about it, you may run her off," Buck advised.

"You're probably right, and I do not want to run her off," Kyle agreed.

He walked the horse to let it cool off and rubbed it down, took gave it a little grain and hay, Buck had made sure of food and water for the rest of the horses, Kyle and Jim usually fed and watered them every day but Sunday, Buck took care of them on Sunday.

Kyle put his tack away, he used his own when he went for rides on Sunday, this was something that Buck respected Kyle for, among other things, the boy respected his property and wouldn't use it even though Buck had told him he could use the ranches in time, Jim was the same way.

"Well, I better be getting home mom well have supper ready," Kyle said.

"It is that time" Buck agreed, "have a good night, see you in the morning," he added.

"You have a good night also and I'll see you in the morning," Kyle replied, with that Kyle headed over the hill to the east where they lived and Buck went into the house.

"I see Kyle was a little bit late today did he have trouble?" His wife, Sally asked.

"Kind of," Buck answered.

"Oh" and what kind of trouble?" Sally asked.

"A young lady on a runaway horse, he managed to catch them," Buck replied.

"That happens as you may recall," Sally said with a smile, she used that trick herself on him and he'd been wise enough to leave it that way," was the girl all right?" She asked.

"Yes," Buck answered, "he stayed with her for a spell to make sure they were all right, turns out that I know the girl's dad, William McFactrick, he's who we got Max from," he added.

"Maybe we should send Kyle up there to see if he has another horse is good is Mac for sale," Sally suggested, "but you're not going up there. I remember his wife Catherin; men can't keep their eyes off her," she explained.

Buck storage suggests he go along then thought he'd not, Sally was all and more woman he needed. "That's a good idea, we can see just how good a horse trader Kyle is," Buck said, "William once he sets a price he will move," he added.

"True Sally agreed," then many times has Mac paid for itself?" She asked.

"Haven't you ever figured, but several times," Buck answered, Mac was some horse.

But this time Kyle came into the house and the first person he came to was Peter.

"Ma Kyle's home," Peter announced, "where have you been Kyle you're late?" He asked.

"All I helped a girl who had a horse go wild," Kyle replied.

"Was she all right," his mother asked.

Yes, I caught her horse after about a mile, we walked to cool it off," Kyle replied.

"Was she pretty," Peter asked.

"Yes," Kyle answered.

"So that's why you're late," Peter surmised.

"Peter when you are Kyle's age you will want to look at girls to," his mother said.

"Why," Peter asked.

"When you're sixteen you think differently about girls," Katie replied.

"Why?" Peter asked.

"When you're sixteen you will know," Katie answered.

"I guess I have to wait that long." Peter asked.

"Yes, we all have to," Kyle replied.

"That will take too long," Peter replied.

"It will be here before you know it," Barnabas said.

"Let's eat," Katie said, they all come to the table and sit down.

"Where did you come across the young lady at?" Barnabas asked.

"Twenty miles west Buck said her dad's name is William Mcfactrick," Kyle answered.

"Don't know him," Barnabas replied.

"Does his wife and daughter both have red hair?" Katie asked.

"I don't know about her mother but she does," Kyle answered.

"I think they both do," Katie said.

"So are you going to take this girl to a dance," Barnabas asked.

"Yes," Kyle answered.

"So you like her," Peter asked.

"Yes I do," Kyle answered.

"When are you going to take her out," Katie asked.

"In two Saturdays I'm going to ask her dad if I can take her out," Kyle said, adding "this Saturday we have a race,"

"Work comes first," Katie said.

"I did tell her I had to work," Kyle explained.

"Don't take too long or someone else will take your place," Katie warned.

"I know," Kyle replied.

Everyone filled their plates and began to eat, shortly after supper Barnabas and the three older boys went to bed, the rest help their mother cleaned up after supper, going to bed shortly after they finished.

Kyle and Jim were up with the sun, their mother was already up and cooking breakfasts, they didn't know how she did it but, she had breakfasts almost done.

Barnabas Jr and their dad came in as Katie was putting breakfasts on the table.

Kyle was thinking about Lillie McFactridge, "not hungry this morning Kyle?" Barnabas asked.

"You, uh" I was thinking of Lillie and didn't see mom put the food down" Kyle replied.

"I see" Barnabas said, adding "they do tell me that girls will do that to you."

"I didn't think they'd take so much of my time," Kyle said.

"He'll get used to it in time," Katie said.

"Maybe so," Kyle said," I better eat and get to work."

"You'll be all right in time," Katie said, after they finished eating they excused their selves and went to work.

Katie was thankful that her boys were able to find work, were they had come from jobs were hard to get, that was why they came to

America and so far they all had been able to get jobs and it was hard for her to believe some of their children were getting girlfriends yet they were of that age.

Kyle and Jim got to work a little before Barnabas Jr and their dad "well you don't look too bad," Buck said.

"Why would I look bad?" Kyle asked.

"You didn't have a girl on your mind last night?" Buck asked.

"Maybe a little," Kyle replied.

"I thought so," Buck said.

"He had a hard time this morning," Jim said, "He about mist breakfasts."

"Oh he's got it bad don't he?" Buck replied.

"I'll be fine," Kyle insisted.

"I know you will," Buck said, "let's get some young ones ready for our riders to ride, to see who they ride the best."

"Start in the second born?" Kyle asked.

"That will be fine," Buck answered, "you two get some of the stock and I'll go get some jockeys."

"Okay will have some in the pins when you get back," Kyle said, they went to the barn, the second one, "you get the first and the fourth horse and I'll get two and the seventh one," Kyle instructed.

"Okay," Jim replied, "what about the third one?"

"Will get him up when we go to the first barn," Kyle said.

"Who do we run him against?" Jim asked

"I decided after a while, probably Mac's two-year-old son," Kyle answered.

"You must think number three is good?" Jim asked.

"We'll see," Kyle replied. They took their first two pare out to the track and tied them up, then got the tact, putting it on number one and five, putting four and seven in the pin close by, they were ready and waiting when the jockeys got there.

The one jockey didn't complain, he rode whatever the best he could, but Jason complained about everything and didn't try his best, so Kyle put Scotty on the best horse.

The first race Jason wined the whole race and loss by 100 feet.

"He could have given you a better race if he had tried," Jim said as they were changing the tact for the next race.

"True," Kyle agreed.

"What was he doing wrong," Buck asked.

"He was too rough and made the horse nervous," Jim answered.

"Kyle anything else," Buck asked.

"He was riding too far forward and the reins were to loose" Kyle replied.

"I didn't see the reins" Buck said.

"They were tucked too far down on his legs," Kyle added.

"They were on his legs," Buck exclaimed, "he knows better than to do that."

"That and all of his weight too far forward takes away their balance," Kyle added.

Buck knew Jason wasn't trying his best, so he went to have a little talk with him, while Buck went to talk to Jason; Kyle and Jim got the other two horses ready to go and were ready at the starting line.

Buck caught up with Jason, "what was wrong was your ride?" Buck asked.

"The horse didn't want to run," Jason replied.

"I'm afraid this time it was the rider who was at fault, not the horse," Buck corrected him, "this time get on the horse set in a right place hold the reins correctly," he directed.

"Yes sir" Jason replied.

"I need to get the best out of the horses so I know which ones to race," Buck said adding "okay?"

"Yes sir," Jason answered, knowing if he wanted to keep his job he better straighten up. Kyle and Jim had the horses ready, this time

Jason set right and had the reins in the right place Kyle dropped the flag and away they went, Jason lost this time to but it was close, only two links.

"Kyle who had the best horse," Buck asked?

"Scotty did," Kyle answered

"Where they that close's," Buck asked?

"Yeah, I'd say they were both riding this time," Kyle answered.

"That was what I thought also," Buck said, "my little talk did some good.

"I'd say so," Kyle agreed. "You and Jim get some more that are close and we'll see if they continue to compete," Buck directed.

"Okay will be back shortly," Kyle said, he and Jim stripped the tack off the last two putting halters and lead ropes back on and took them back to the barn and brought two more pair, nine, six, eight and twelve, all of these were very close and it shows in the first pair, Jason won by a nose.

They ran five more races that day and they were a lot better though Scotty won six out of the eight races but, most of them were by a head, and that was how it went the rest of the week, every day they ran eight races Scotty did win most of them and once again they were very close, by a head or a half-link.

On Thursday they had Scotty to ride Maxes colt up against Bucks next fastest horse that wasn't kin to Max and Scotty and Max Junior won by five links, Jason was holding his head down when he rode up.

"Don't be too hard on yourself Jason, that colt is just that fast," Kyle explained.

"The one I was on isn't slow," Jason exclaimed.

"The rider and the horse are a team and some horses stand out above the rest," Kyle explained, "his comes from his bloodline, and the truth is I thought he would have beat you by twice what he did," this made Jason feel better but not a lot.

After the week of riding they learned that the riders were very close to the same in their abilities, the difference was Scotty was happy-go-lucky win or lose, while Jason showed his anger when he lost.

"What do you think Kyle?" Buck asked.

"They are very close, though Scotty will out ride Jason," Kyle explained.

"Okay why do you say that? They both ride very good after the little talk I had with Jason," Buck asked.

When Jason loses, the next horse feels his anger, horses feel your moods, Scotty doesn't change like Jason, you see how he bulls up and when he does that the horse feels his tension," Kyle explained further.

"I see what you mean I think," Buck said," one rides a horse the other becomes one with the horse," he explained.

"Now you see," Kyle said, "horses know our moods, they do most of the work but, we help a little," he explained.

"Well let's put them up and tomorrow we will ride each of them to keep them limber but, no racing them," Buck directed.

"Jim let's put these up and get the feeding done."

As they were doing their chores for the day Buck rode one of his gentler, less muscle smoother geldings and went up on the hill overlooking the pasture overlooking the mares and colts, this crop of colts definitely had a more muscular look to their frame, this was due to Max fathering them for the most part, some of the others were fathered by Buck old stud; the one that Jason ran against Max Jr. earlier in the week, Buck was very pleased with what he saw, even the ones from his older stallion that he used on a few of his heavier muscled mares looked very good.

The boys were just finishing up feeding and putting things up for the day as he rode up, "y'all about done for the day," Buck asked.

"Yes," Kyle answered.

"Good, now tomorrow y'all take the seven fastest horses and walked them around the track a few times so they'll be fresh Saturday,"

Buck instructed them "let Jim ride them as he is closer to the weight of the jockeys."

"All right will be here first thing in the morning," Kyle replied.

"Now be thinking about horses the next couple of days, not ladies," Buck teased.

"We'll do our best to," Kyle said.

Buck laughed and said, "I know you will, good night."

"Good night," they both replied, and headed home.

Kyle had been working hard with the horses but, often Lillie came to the front of his mind and he would have to put her in the back and his mine back on the horses.

"It's hard to keep your mind on the jobs with the pretty girl there ain't it," Jim stated.

"Yes they do pop up from time to time," Kyle responded.

"Nancy does that a lot," Jim agreed.

"Yes she's a nice lady though more like a sister to me," Kyle said.

"That's kind of like what she said about you," Jim said, "said you're always here and help her when she goes ride a horse you got it ready for her and always put it up."

"I suppose that's a different kind of loving someone," Kyle pointed out.

"I see what you mean," Jim replied, it's like loving someone in your family but you're not in love with them."

"Yes you have it," Kyle agreed.

"What do you think about the riders for the horses?" Jim asked.

"They're both very capable riders," Kyle answered.

"But," Jim asked?

"Scott is a better rider of the two because he and the horses get along better," Kyle explained.

"It's like when he loses the horses is still his best friend," Jim said.

"That's what makes him the better rider," Kyle agreed, "He just loves horses."

"You're the same way," Jim stated.

"Well maybe a little," Kyle said, "mines somewhat like an instructor, stricter than Scotty's."

"Yeah yours is like a father to a son, Scotty's is like to a best friend," Jim replied.

"Something like that," Kyle agreed.

Kyle was growing up fast for a young man, Buck had seen this two years ago, most people want to get through the day and go home, Kyle was thinking about tomorrow and the next day and the next day. Jim was getting a little like that but, not there yet, Kyle was thanking what to do best, see before the race are after, while Jim was thinking make sure they get fed today, to some it sounds the same, but isn't, too much is as bad is not enough, Jim would get a lesson on that the next few days and he was learning and he wanted not to just impress Kyle, Buck and his family but, he wanted to learn, Kyle and Buck told him if you will you can learn everyday if you don't you just wasted a day.

Kyle and Jim were home in time for supper right after their father and brothers, they were cleaning up, they had to bathe everyday to get the coal dust off, Kyle and Jim had to or their mother would not let them in the house she said they smelled like a horse.

After cleaning up they had supper and talked about their day, the mine was hard and dusty work, loading coal all day, taking care of horses was a lot cleaner you had to clean out the barn stalls everyday but, it wasn't as hard or dirty as other work.

Some men like work that was hard and some men didn't, just as in their family they were split on what they like, it all takes muscles just different ones for the most part and dirt, the mines were a lot dirtier.

"How is the horse racing preparing going," Katie asked.

"Going good now that we have the riders working at it," Kyle stated.

"I thought y'all always had two?" Barnabas asked.

"We do but, only one was putting out any effort," Jim explained.

"Oh, what was his problem?" Katie asked. "Not sure if it was he thought he was always going to get the slowest horse or he just didn't care," Kyle answered.

"And," Barnabas asked.

"He straightened out after Buck pointed out that he wasn't trying and that he needed his best effort," Kyle answered.

"He's still not as good as Scotty," Jim added.

"Some people are more suitable for some jobs," Katie pointed out.

"That's true, how they treat the horses has a lot to do with how well they do," Jim said.

"Did someone tell you this are did you figure it out for yourself?" His dad asked.

"Some of both," Jim answered.

"Sounds like you're learning," Barnabas remarked.

"Yeah but, I have a lot to learn yet," Jim replied.

"If we will we'll learn every day," Katie stated.

"I think I have a lot to learn," Jim stated.

"Not just you son," Barnabas said adding, "There is always something to learn."

"When we think we've got something figured out, something happens that makes us feel like we don't know anything," Kyle said.

"Yes but even Buck asked you things," Jim said.

"Just with horses, there is a whole world out there for me to learn," Kyle explained.

"Son some people are good at some things like Kyle is with horses and when Buck sees that he learned, it's best to ask their advice to help them see things they messed," Barnabas said.

"You're saying when I don't understand I should ask," Jim asked.

"Isn't that what you just said Buck does to Kyle?" Barnabas asked.

"I suppose," Jim answered.

"Don't you think it helps him do a better job and maybe his questions help Kyle do better?" Barnabas asked.

"I hadn't thought of that," Jim said, "you're saying sometimes his questions are to help Kyle do better right?"

"Could be that or to see if they agree with each other," Barnabas explained.

"Most of the time it's to see if they agree I think," Jim said to which they all laughed.

It wasn't too long after supper they all went to bed work would come around soon enough in the morning and it would be another hard day and long.

CHAPTER 2

The next morning Katie was up before daylight and started breakfast with the smell of coffee and cooking the rest started getting up and getting dressed for the day, it would be a hard day for both those that where coal miner's and getting the horses ready to race.

One by one they started coming to the table to eat, it wouldn't be long before they headed to work, Barnabas and Barnabas Jr. would be going to the mine, while Kyle and Jim to the horse farm.

Kyle would be doing the feeding, Jim would be watching and learning, later he would be riding them to keep them fresh though they had a big day tomorrow, horses were not what was on Kyle's mind this morning, she was beautiful with red hair and a full bloomed woman, she'd have to give room to his job shortly as hard as it is sometimes for him to concentrate.

They finished breakfast and headed for the jobs after thanking their mother and saying goodbye.

Barnabas lingered and gave Katie a kiss, "you've raised some fine young boys Hun," Barnabas praised her. "We," she corrected him, "raise some fine boys," she added.

"Well I may have helped a little bit, most of the time it was you, I was at work," Barnabas said.

"Which is where you better go before you're late," Katie pointed out.

"Yes dear love you," Barnabas said. "I love you too, bye Hun." Katie replied. With a wave he headed to work to start the new day.

"So you have her picture in your mind this morning," Jim stated after they left their dad and brother.

"And how did you know?" Kyle asked.

"You had that faraway look in your eye this morning that and you haven't said much," Jim answered.

"Buck's daughter, is she on your mind a lot?" Kyle asked.

"All the time," Jim answered.

"I look for her all the time, like when I'm in the barn she comes in for a horse to ride I saddle the horse for her to ride," Kyle explained, "it's funny I'm been around her a lot and I've got her a lot of horses to ride but, I've never looked at her the way I look at Lillie, I have Lillie on my mind all the time.

"I guess it's who appeals to us," Jim said.

"Yes I think it's true when I saw Lillie it was love at first sight," Kyle said, "but today we better have our eyes on the horses."

"Yes," Jim answered, "and I hope in time I can learn horses like you have."

"Each one is like a book, you have to read them," Kyle replied.

"Well I hope I can learn horse," Jim added.

"You already have and will," Kyle stated. They got to the barn at the same time as Buck.

"Good morning," they all said.

"You want to ride the horses this morning Kyle?" Buck asked.

"I thought you said yesterday you want Jim to ride them?" Kyle asked.

"Oh that's right," Buck replied, "That Way, Jim will get some education."

"So to speak," Kyle replied, "and you said that Jim was closer to the Jockey's size,"

"I think it is a good ideal, also you give him some pointers along the way on what to look for," Buck said, "for him, and the horses of course."

"Okay, Jim start in here on the right number four if the horse even at a walk isn't smooth, let's say choppy you are the saddles not in the right place, Kyle began, "this one the saddle needs to be a little bit forward, how you set will make a difference in the smoothness," thus began Jim's education for the day.

Jim learn this horse was smoother if he set forward on him but, the next one slow down or raised his head if you lean forward, by adjusting the saddle back and leaning a little bit forward he was smoother and picked up his walk, he learned right away that his assumption that horses were all horses went out to window after just two horses, they were just like humans in that they had their own personalities, if anything humans just had more differences is all, if anything this got him to pay more attention to each horse, and one-day he learned a lot, not all he needed but, a good start.

Kyle feed the horses differently, Jim noticed some he gave less hay and more grain, to others he gave more hay and less grain but, not all they want and he knew he'd give them some more tonight and a little in the morning, he didn't know how Kyle figured it out, he hoped he'd teach him how.

Jim rode each one around the track, slow at first then a fast walk, last he'd get off and walk to cool them off, it made for a long day and was good for the horses, when he came to Max Jr. it was like getting on a different animal and when he let him get up some speed felt like floating, unreal the different to Jim, he had to pull to get him down to a walk.

When he walked him to the barn Kyle asks, "Hard to believe the power in him?"

"There's no other like him," Jim replied.

"There's one," Kyle corrected.

"Who," Jim demanded.

"Max," Kyle answered, adding, "I believe Max is faster by a little and he has six one year olds and more on the way with potential,"

"Will they be as fast?" Jim ask. "Some will, some won't, their mother's make a differents on how they do," Kyle answered.

"Well his first one is a runner," Jim stated.

"That he is," Kyle agreed "he your last one?"

"Yeah," Jim answered.

"Ok you get a bucket of feed and I'll give each one a little," Kyle said.

"Okay," Jim replied. They finest out the day feeding the horses and Buck meet them as they were coming out the door.

Well what do you think?" Buck asks.

"I think Jim learned a little about horses today," Kyle replied.

"Oh?" Buck inquired.

"I've a ways to go yet," Jim replied.

"Yes but, he learned a lot, I seen you adjust the saddle and the chinch and how you set, and held the reins," Kyle praised.

"True," Jim agreed, "But I know there's more."

"Not as much as you think," Buck said. Jim had a look on his face of disbelief.

"He's right," Kyle said, "finding the comfort of the horse is the key, like what you're doing today."

"Okay," Jim replied.

"I hope you remember some of what you learned today," Buck said adding, "We'll be asking you."

"Oh man! I don't know if I can," he explained.

"Don't worry you'll do fine," Buck assured him. "I hope so," Jim said. Kyle and Buck laughed.

"Let's go homes so you can get a good night's sleep," Kyle suggested.

"I hope I can sleep," Jim replied mostly to his self.

"Don't worry Jim you'll get it in time," Buck said, "goodnight."

"Goodnight," both boys' said, as they headed home, Buck was still chuckling when he went into the house.

"What are you chuckling about?" Beth asks him.

"Oh we were teasing Jim a little about his schooling on horse and he thinks he has to remember everything he learned today," Buck explained.

"You don't learn horse in one day," Beth said, "don't run him away."

"No way," Buck said, "anyway he's not going anywhere, there is another interest here."

"Yes I know and you make sure he stays," Kathy replied.

"Don't worry he's not going anywhere," Buck assured her, "I watched him today and he's been paying attention to Kyle and he learned a lot."

"Is he as sharp as Kyle," Catherine asked."

"Only time will tell that," Buck answered, "but I will say he definitely has promise."

Their dad and Barnabas were washing off when they got home, only this time they were a lot blacker than usual.

"How come y'all are so dirty?" Jim asked.

"We had some roof fall twice," Barnabas answered.

"Anyone get hurt?" Kyle asked.

"No," Barnabas answered adding, "but it was very close when it fell the second time, to close.

"That's why we are so dirty," Barnabas Jr. explained.

"Our boss is saying there's talk of getting something that hits the roof and knocks loose stuff down," Barnabas said.

"I hope so," Kyle said, "Did he say anything about cutting down the dirt or dust?"

"They haven't said too much about the dust and they have tried a few things, with very little improvement," Barnabas replied.

"I hope they do," Jim said, "it can't be good to breath that much dust in."

"I think you're right son," Barnabas agreed.

"Y'all all ready for race day?" Barnabas Jr. asked.

"Yeah and so are the horses," Kyle answered.

"I'm not," Jim said, "Buck said he was going to ask me some questions about the horses tomorrow and I can't remember anything."

"Don't worry Jim he won't be hard on you, he just wants to help you learn more about horses," Kyle explained, "he does the same to me it helps me learn more about horses."

"I sure hope you're right," Jim worried.

"Don't worry, you'll remember tomorrow more than you think you will," Kyle assured him.

"I don't know I've been trying but it won't come in my head," Jim said.

"What made lighten run faster?" Kyle asked.

"Oh," I don't, "oh! I mowed to Saddle back and leaned forward," he answered.

"See you'll do fine," Kyle said.

"Even if you don't remember everything tomorrow you will remember it in time," Barnabas Jr. said.

"I guess so," Jim said.

"You two are next," Katie informed them.

"Okay mom we know," Kyle said.

"Can't go out in public looking like bums, right," Jim added.

"See you're already learned," Barnabas Jr. said.

"Yeah," his dad said.

"I guess life is just like a big school," Jim stated.

"Now you're learning," his dad said, "and when you're old and gray you'll still be learning it doesn't stop."

"I hope it's not all this hard," Jim replied.

"It's not," Barnabas assured him, "it doesn't go away and when you're young you have so many things to learn at least we think we do, some things are needed and some we'll never use and we pick up a few things along the way we use all the time."

All the boys believed what their dad was saying and saw the wisdom in it, by the time Kyle and Jim got cleaned up Katie called them in to supper.

After they set down Barnabas said grace, then it was time for questions and Peter was full of them.

"Why did the roof fall down," Peter asked.

"Sometimes when you break the coal when it falls loose stuff stays in the ceiling," Barnabas answered. "Well why doesn't it all fall down," Peter asked.

"It's like this room have walls and you have boards across it to hold everything up above it," Barnabas Jr. answered.

"God holds it up," one of his younger sisters said.

"How come he lets some of fall?" Peter asked.

"Some of it slips through his fingers," his brother said.

"This seemed to satisfied Peter on the falling coal he went from that to why they were black when they came home, then he went to the horses did they race? Who won? Who rode the horse? Why did Jim ride the horses and not Kyle? It made supper go by very quickly and soon after they finished eating the boys went to bed, Barnabas stayed in the kitchen talking to Katie for a while, she was concerned about what would've happened if the coal would've fallen on them.

"Wouldn't have been good, at the least broken bones, and I think you know the worst,

"Isn't there something they can do to make it safer?" Katie asked.

"Well I think they are actually checking and to doing just that," Barnabas began, "our boss has been talking to other people in the quarry business and they're trying to find a device that knocks the loose stuff off the ceiling looking into better shoring up the walls but you know we can't afford to cover the whole thing, but I think this machine chips loose stuff down is the best idea."

I wish you could find a better way to make a living," Katie said, "I worry about all of you but, I think you and Barnabas have the most dangerous job." Barnabas couldn't argue about that, he kissed her and said, "We're in God's hands."

She knew that but she still worried and prayed to God morning and night for their safety, with the kiss Barnabas went off to bed, tomorrow was come early, with them shoring up were the coal fall today.

After Katie got the rest of the family to bed she went and prayed to God for their safety and thanked Him for watching over them, Katie was a strong believer in God and she knew that without any doubt that God could answer her prayers she guess it was just the fight that went on with Satan that caused the worry, she also knew that Barnabas was a strong believer and also asking and thanked God regularly.

She went around the kitchen making sure everything was put away, she washed her hands and face and went to bed.

"If nothing else Peter keeps our minds thinking with his questions," Barnabas said, as Katie was climbing into bed.

"It must be something we need or God wouldn't have given him to us," Katie stated.

"I think his questions make me look more closely at the ceilings and walls and other dangers at work," Barnabas said.

"Well don't hurry and hurt someone," Katie replied.

"I think that is very good advice, not only do I have me and my son's life to look after but in a way everyone's at the quarry, I am not a boss, just a old hand," Barnabas said, and not to leave you out I had to come home and see you."

"Oh I do matter," Katie stated.

"Very much my dear, we'd be lost without you," Barnabas praised.

"As we'd be lost without you," Katie replied, they hugged then became quiet after that, sometimes words are not necessary for two people who love each other as they did, they went to sleep in each other's arms.

CHAPTER 3

RACE DAY

After a quiet night Katie was the first one up with Barnabas and then the three oldest boy's right behind him, Katie had gotten up a little bit earlier this morning knowing that Kyle and Jim had to be at work at daylight to get everything prepared to go to the races, it would be a long day for them.

They were getting the horses harnessed and ready when Buck came to the barn.

"Good morning," Buck said.

"Good morning Buck," they said in return.

"Looks like it's going to be a pretty day for racing," Buck predicted, "hope the jockeys have their heads on straight."

"Oh I think they will," Kyle predicted."

"Do you remember anything about the horses Jim?" Buck asked.

"Yes sir I think I do," Jim answered.

"Good," Buck said, "you'll be getting them set up with Kyle watching you okay."

Seeing the worrying in Jim's eyes did not worry Buck too much, "don't worry I don't expect you to remember everything in one day," Buck explained, "you have to start somewhere though and besides Kyle will be helping you."

"I know, it's I don't want to disappoint you though," Jim replied.

"You won't," Buck said, "let's get them on a string and ready to head out, as soon as we get the wagon loaded with tact," while Kyle and Jim were loading the tact Buck called for his wife and daughter to get in the wagon it was time to go, and off to the races they headed.

Buck entered eight races putting Max Junior in three of them he put Scotty on him twice and Jason as rider in one giving him a chance on him to see how he did, this would be the first time Max Junior ran in competition.

Kyle thought there would be some surprise folks here today he had not seen anyone else with a horse at any of the other races like Max Junior, no one had come close to Max Senior in any of the races that he ran in time would tell.

Usually Kyle set them up but today Jim was setting up the horses for racing and Kyle was overseeing, a little later in the morning Buck asked how Jim was doing?

"He is doing real well," Kyle said, "I've seen him make two mistakes, and he corrected them without me telling him."

"Good, good." Buck replied.

On their first race Bucks horses came in second and third the second race Scotty on one of his young studs won, the third Jason won on Max Jr. and he had a smile on his face a mile wide, on his next race he lost by a nose but he was still smiling, at the end of the race Max Jr. won all three of his last two with Scotty riding him and he won with a large distance between him and the nearest competitor, he was as strong on his last race as he was in his first one, his other horses came in second in two other races, with a third place in another, all said it was a very good day, and as Kyle thought, Max Jr. shined as the fastest horse present.

When they got home they were some happy people, "I want to congratulate all of you Scotty and Jason for an excellent job of riding, Jim for the sendups, Kyle for the teaching a overseeing the setups, and my family for their support," Buck said, adding after this performance today the only sad part is its three weeks to the next race."

Kyle was thinking he could go to Lillie's on the next Saturday that was on his mind she was thinking of him what he was doing and wishing next Saturday was here.

At the William's farm, "what are you thinking about Lillie?" her mother asked her.

"Wishing it was next Saturday," Lillie replied.

"Oh a boy," Catherine quizzed.

"Not just any boy," Lillie answered.

"I know, one you think is tall and handsome," Catherine said, "that the one on your mind?"

"Was it like that for you with dad?" Lillie asked, changing the subject.

"Yes, her mother replied.

"Good I thought I was going crazy," Lillie said.

"Why's that?" She asked, "are you thinking about wanting to kiss this boy?"

"Mother," Lillie exclaimed.

"Well," her mother asked again.

"Yes." She answered.

"I thought so, that was what I thought about when I met your dad," Catherine explained, "it was a while before I found out it was wonderful and worth the wait, even better than I thought."

"Oh?" Lillie asked.

"But, young lady first you make sure he's the right one before you'll pass the kiss," her mother instructed her.

"Yes mama, it's just I've never had anyone make me feel like this," Lillie replied.

"I thought perhaps you may not be like me, but there's no hope for him," her mother said, "he couldn't run fast enough to get away from you if they wanted to, not that he wants to."

"But mother he is so handsome," Lillie began, her mother raised her hand.

"I have seen him in town and I know who his mother is, a good woman, but get to know him first and make sure your heart agrees with your eyes," Catherine advise.

Lillie thought that was good advice, a present can be wrapped beautifully do not have anything inside of beauty or good, she would see.

Kyle and Jim went about putting the horses in there pins, feeding the stock and putting away the tack, after Buck paid the jockeys he came back into the barn.

"Boys a lot of this winning today was you're doing, how you feed them how you take care of them and the paying attention to them," Buck praised.

"Kyle is the one who does all that," Jim replied.

"Who set them up today?" Kyle asked.

"Both of you helped, Jim how do you thank Kyle knows how to do what he does?" Buck asked.

"I suppose by doing it so long," Jim answered.

"That is part of it," Buck began, adding "there are some who work with horses who never learn the way you two have."

"What do you mean?" Jim asked.

"What did you learn yesterday?" Buck asked.

"Ways to make the horse run faster for one," Jim answered.

"That's right that's part of it," Buck agreed, "what did Kyle do Friday?"

"He fed them differently," Jim replied.

"Right again," Buck answered, "most people let them have all the hay they want and too much grain and then their full and won't give their best," he explained.

"I see, I think, yeah after I ate a big meal I don't want to jump on a horse and ride fast," Jim replied.

"The horse that is full doesn't want to be riding his fastest either," Kyle added.

"I see what you mean," Jim said.

"If there full and say and a person sets on them they don't do their best," Buck said.

"And if their full it doesn't matter where you set on them," Jim added.

"I think the light has come on," Kyle said "I believe so," Buck said smiling.

"I'm a little slow," Jim began.

"You're by no means slow Jim, you're doing real fine keep up the good work," Buck praised.

"As I said we learn all the time." Kyle reminded him.

"I know," Jim said, "I'm just impatient and want to know everything now."

"We all do, it just doesn't happen that way," Buck said, "after you get everything put up and fed, y'all can go home, once again good job and I'll go out in the pastures check the stock, an y'all can have the rest of today off."

"Okay thanks," they replied." "Oh, what were you going to ride tomorrow Kyle?" Buck asked.

"I hadn't thought that far," Kyle said.

"Why don't you come and get Coaly and take her up to Lillie's dad tomorrow and see how much to have his best stud breed her," Buck suggested.

A smile came to Kyle's face, "I would be glad to," Kyle replied.

"Okay after church come and get her," Buck said, "Oh remember she's not kin to Max, he'll need to know that."

"I'll remember and thank you," Kyle said.

"You're welcome," Buck replied, "I am going to go look at the cows, see you two in the morning."

"Bye," they both said. They fed the horse's grain and hay and Jim noticed Kyle gave them more today than Friday.

"How come you give them all more today than yesterday?" Jim asked.

"They're not racing tomorrow are for three weeks," Kyle answered, "plus I'm giving them a treat for a job well done."

"They did do that," Jim agreed, "and time may be I'll get the way you treat horses different figured out."

"Don't worry, just watch and pay attention to the way I feed them as I watched Buck and learned what to look for, the things he showed me," Kyle explained.

"I know it takes time to learn," Jim stated, "I just want to know it all now." "I don't know it all by a longshot, you just keep trying," Kyle said, "it's like each horse has its own personality and you have to learn it."

"Yes but, you know a lot and what's more how to unlock their personality," Jim pointed out.

"You will in time," Kyle assured him, "look at all you learn this past week, don't try to measure yourself by what you learn but, that you're learning and be grateful," he advised him.

"I guess that's true," Jim replied. They finished taking care of the horses and Jim went to the house to tell his girlfriend bye and Kyle went home, the thought of seeing Lillie was on his mind, he would definitely have to clean up good tonight when he got home, Pete seen him and came running.

"Did you win?" was Peter's first question.

"Some of the horses won," Kyle answered.

"Did Max win?" He asked.

"Yes he did, he won three races," Kyle answered, they were close to the house.

"You did good?" Katie asked.

"Yeah," Kyle replied, "we won five out of eight and came in second in two others."

"That is good," Katy praised.

"I'm going to clean up," Kyle began, "oh has dad come home yet?"

"No not yet," Katie answered, "you have a date tonight?" She asked.

"No I just have an errand to run for Buck tomorrow is all," Kyle replied.

"Oh I see," Katie said.

Knowing he couldn't keep it away from his mother he explained, "I'm going to take a mare to Lillie's dad to see how much he'll charge to breed her to his best stud."

"OH" I see," Katie said and ask, "after church I hope?"

"Yeah." Kyle answered.

"She'll still be there when you get there," Katie assured him. "I know she will," Kyle said. Peter had wandered off on another adventure.

"I remember the first time I saw your father, he was all I could see after that," Katie said.

"Lillie is always on my mind, see pops up everywhere," he said.

"If she is the one she'll always be there," Katie said adding, "your father is not far away in mine."

"Sense I laid my eyes on Lillie, I have all but forgot the dream of the wild West," Kyle said.

"She may be all the wild you can handle," his mother teased.

"She may be all the wild I want," Kyle pointed out.

"She is and will be more important than any wild adventure," Katie explained, "where is your brother did Jim get lost," she asked.

"He's still at Bucks," Kyle answered.

"A young lady perhaps," She inquired.

"Yes when I left he was headed to the house," Kyle explained.

"I first thought he'd be the first to merry but, now I'm not so sure," Katie said.

"Time will tell mother," Kyle said, "I'm going to go take a bath," Katie hoped that Lillie could hold him.

"Okay, don't take too long I'm sure your dad and Barnabas will be home soon," Katie replied.

Kyle went and took a bath he was thankful that his mother had put some water in the kettle to heat. The other kids were playing, the girls with dolls and the boys with ropes and stick horses, Peter was trying to rope his older brother, he wasn't having much luck but it didn't stop him from trying.

Jim came home later and he tried to help Peter by showing him how to hold the rope and turned it over his head, it helped a little.

"I'll never get it," Peter said.

"Sure you will Peter, you keep trying it will come to you," Jim assured him.

Jim went into the house, "hello mother," Jim said.

"Well hello Jim," Katie replied, "I hear the horses did very well today."

"Yes they did, even better than we thought they would," he said.

"Kyle said you stopped at the house before you came home," Katie asked.

"Yes I told Becky bye before I left," Jim explained.

"And how is she?" She asked.

"Oh she's fine," Jim answered, "excited about the races."

"I hope you told her she's more than just fine," his mother said.

"Yes I did," he replied.

"That's good," Katie said, "we girls may know how you men feel but we still like to hear it."

"We can't be around dad without learning a little mom," Jim said." "I see," Katie said, "take a bath before your dad and brother get home," she insisted.

"Yes mother, I had planned on it," Jim replied. He went and got his water ready, filled a bucked black up and put a little water back in the kettle for them, got in, then as he was finishing up his dad and brother came home, there were almost black again today from work, they had been working on the roof putting timbers in place and taking poles knocking the loose parts of the roof down, it was dirty work. Their dad was as dirty today as Barnabas Jr. he had helped clean up the fall today instead of working on the plant like normal.

He told Katie later he wanted to make sure their son was working safely and he was, after they had cleaned up Katie told the younger ones to get ready for supper, she was about ready to put supper on the table.

"Is this how black people gets black?" Peter asked.

"I don't think so," Katie answered.

Well how do they," Peter asked adding don't they start out white?"

"No," Barnabas answered, "God made us different colors when he made man and no I don't know why?"

"Maybe He did it to better tell us apart," Peter suggested.

"Maybe," Katie replied.

"How come they made their coal black so we could tell it from dirt?" Peter asked.

"And rocks," Barnabas Jr said.

"How come," Peter asked?

"Rocks won't burn like coal," Barnabas Jr replied.

"But trees will and there green, how come they will," Peter asked?

"There are lots of things that will burn Peter," his dad said.

"Oh," Peter said, "like what?"

"Oil will and you can put it on the axle of your wood box to keep it cool," Barnabas Jr said.

"How can it do that," Peter asked?

"If you put it on an axle it doesn't get hot enough to burn but if you light a match to it, it does," Barnabas Jr explained.

"Really how come," Peter asked?

"Okay Peter let it rest, so we all can eat," Katie directed.

"Okay," Peter said, adding "I still don't understand though."

"You will give yourself time to learn," Jim advised him.

"You're always in a hurry," his oldest sister said.

"So," Peter replied.

"You two stop fighting and start eating," Katie told them.

So they stopped and started eating, it took a lot of food for three grown boys plus the other four children, fortunately they had been blessed with good jobs so they were doing well, when they took the chance of coming here they didn't know what they were in for, so far it had turned out so much better than they expected and never dreamed possible, they were very blessed.

As night came on they helped their mother clean up after supper, the younger ones took a bath and then went to bed, and shortly thereafter they were all in bed with good nights said.

"Kyle tell you what he is doing tomorrow," Katie asked.

"No, he didn't mention anything," Barnabas answered.

"He's taking a mare up to the Mcfactrick to see how much it will cost to have her bred," Katie explained.

"Wait a minute, isn't that where the young lady lives," Barnabas asked?

"One and the same," Katie answered.

"Well it sounds like our son is looking at a different kind of wild area," Barnabas suggested.

He made some mention of that this afternoon," Katie said, "something about she was all he could think of."

"I know there was a time there wasn't anyone but you in my thoughts, then our kids came along and had to make room for them, though you were always there somewhere, Barnabas said.

"I told him if she's the one she'll stay on his mind," Katie said.

"Well good night honey, see you in my dreams," Barnabas said."

"Good night," Katie replied chuckling.

The next morning everyone was up early and getting ready for church, Kyle was the first one to leave going to Bucks to hook up the coach then getting it in front of house just as they were coming out.

"Good morning Kyle," they all said. "Good morning how are y'all doing this morning," Kyle inquired?

"Just fine," Buck said, "and you."

"Fine," Kyle answered.

"They were getting into the coach and Becky had to go back in the house, she had forgotten her Bible, after a few minutes she returned and got in, Buck shut the door.

"Okay let's go Kyle," Buck instructed.

With a flip of the reins away they went, it wasn't too awful far but, it still took a half hour to get there, they arrived just behind Kyle's parents and family and they went in together.

The preachers talk was on family and marriage and faithfulness to each other, the very thing that was on some of the youngsters' minds, a mate and marriage, there comes a time.

After church and after saying goodbye to everyone, Kyle drove them home, put the coach up, Kyle being invited to the dinner with them did and then he saddled the mare and was on his way to the McFactrick, it would be a long ride, it was uneventful but, in his mind all he could think of was Lillie and how beautiful she was, finally came to their winter home but, no one was there so he follow the trail to their home that they spent the summer in, and made the top across the pasture to the house were Lillie and her mother were outside.

"Good afternoon ma'am, Lillie," Kyle said.

"Hello," Lillie replied, Kyle could see were Lillie got her beauty from after seeing her mother. "Mother this is Kyle, Kyle this is my mother," she introduced.

"Hello," they both said, "I actually came out today for two reasons, one to ask permission to see Lillie, and the other my boss wanted me to ask your husband about getting this mare bred to his best stud," Kyle explained.

"Why don't you get down and I'll go find him," Catherine said.

"Yes ma'am," Kyle answered, "hi Lillie."

"Hello Kyle," Lillie replied, as her mother went around the house.

"You look very pretty today," Kyle complemented her.

"Thank you," Lillie replied, "you look very fine today yourself, I wasn't expecting you today."

"I wasn't expecting to get here but, my boss ask me yesterday afternoon to ride this mare up here and talk to your dad, and I said yes I would be very glad to have the reason to come see you," Kyle explained.

"I'm very glad you came," Lillie said.

"Every sense I put my eyes on you last week you're on my mind all of the time," Kyle said.

"I know the feeling and I'm very glad you came," Lillie said, "my mom just tease me, said my body is her that I mind isn't." They both laughed.

"I'm not a man of a lot of words, I work around horses mostly but I will never have anyone stirred me like you," Kyle said.

"Oh I think I know what you mean, I just like to be around you," Lillie stated.

"I definitely do like that, I guess that's the difference between love and like," Kyle said.

"I guess so, did you all go to the races," Lilly asked?

"Yes," Kyle answered, "we, my bosses horses won five out of eight of the races, one horse won three races, he is a colt out of one of your dad's horses," he explained.

"He must be very fast," Lillie stated. "He is though he can't stay up with his dad Max." Kyle explained.

"I remember him," Lillie stated, "how come your boss wants to breed this mare to something else," she asked?

"He'd like to try a different horse from a different line," Kyle explained.

"I'd have thought he'd want to breed them all to Max," Lillie asked.

"We have done that with a lot with the blood and build for racing, I think he's looking for another Max," Kyle said.

"So he can keep winning," Lillie said, "I think I see his thinking,"

"I'm not used to talking to girls so such, what do you like," Kyle asked?

"For one horses, I like all kinds of animals," Lillie answered.

"I do to," Kyle said, "did you ever see the longhorn cattle pictures from Texas," he asked.

"Yes, how about the Porky Pines," Lilly asked?

"In pictures," Kyle answered.

"Me too, I bet they hurt if they poke you," Lillie replied.

"Yeah with all those needles," Kyle agreed.

"Here's dad," Lillie said pointing toward the house he was coming around the house.

"Hello," Kyle said.

"Hello, my wife says Buck sent you to ask about having a mare bred," William asked?

"That and one question for myself," Kyle replied?

"Oh she mentioned that to," he replied, "you been helping Buck long?"

"Yes I went to work for him right before he bought Max," Kyle answered.

"Well what's on your mind," William asked, knowing what he wanted.

"Well sir I like to ask your permission to take Lillie on a date," Kyle stated.

"I see, well let's see you have a job, and I suppose if you get serious you could take care of her," Williams said.

"Yes sir," Kyle answered.

"I guess so but take it slow Lillie, don't rush into anything," he decided, "now about the horse?" Kyle pointed at the red mare, "Buck wanted to know how much it would cost to breed her to your best stud," Kyle asked.

"Oh, tell him Twenty five dollars," Williams said.

"Ok I'll tell him when I get back," Kyle replied, "Thank you."

"Nice to meet you," William said.

"You to Sir," Kyle replied.

"William is my name," he added.

"Kyle is mine, Kyle O'Rielly," Kyle introduces his self.

Lillie's mother came around the house, "would you like some cake young man," Catharine ask.

"Yes thank you," Kyle answered.

"Come in the house," Lillie invited.

"Lead the way," Kyle said. They all went in and got a piece of cake and a glass of tea, it was good, very nice.

"Thank you it was good," Kyle praise."

"You're welcome," Catherine said, "Lillie why don't you get your horse and ride down as far as the other house when he goes home," she suggested.

"Let Kyle saddle her and will see what kind of a horse man he is," her dad suggested.

Lillie got a worried look on her face but, Kyle said "lead the way," which she did. For once her dad received a surprise, Lillie's mare only allowed a select few to touch her, she rarely allows him.

Kyle took the bridle, blanket and saddle into the lot and walked right up to her mare and put the bridle in her mouth which she accepted without any problem, he talked to her the whole time, he then put the blanket on and then the saddle, then leading her to a smiling Lillie.

"My brothers won't get close to her and she just barely allows dad," Lillie explained, "and seeing you walk right up to her it's hard to believe."

"My voice seems to calm animals," Kyle said.

Lillie thought for a second and replied, "me too."

"If I had not seen it I would not have believed it," her dad said.

"You know your brothers will not believe it," her mother said, "there are very few people we can do that, now don't you be gone too long Lillie."

"Yes mom," Lillie replied.

"By and thank you for the cake it was good and I'll tell Buck oh, he told me to tell you that this mare is no kin to max," Kyle said.

"I wondered she's built some like him," William said.

"No they are not kin, she's from his old stock, her dad was one of Bucks best horses before Max," Kyle explained.

"Before Max," He questioned?

"We've nothing that can touch him though one of his sons can stay with him but, he can't best him," Kyle explained.

"He must have muscled some," Williams said, "does he get a lot of grain?"

"We give him some everyday, plus before a race week cut his hay which helps his speed, we very the feed it depending upon the build of the individual horses, most people won't run against Max, yesterday we ran his two-year-old son in three races he won all three," Kyle answered.

"I didn't know that would make a lot of difference," Williams stated.

"It doesn't make a lot of difference but, when you have two horses that are very even and makes enough difference to win," Kyle explained.

"Tell your boss that this stud will be a half-brother to Max," Williams said, "I believe he'd still give Max a run for his money and he's had very little grain."

"Okay I'll tell him," Kyle replied, "it was nice to meet y'all today."

"It was nice to meet you too Kyle," William replied, "Now don't keep my daughter gone for too long."

"Yes sir I won't," Kyle assured him.

"Bye," they all said as Kyle and Lillie road away down the trail. Lillie was more impressed each time she met Kyle.

After they got out of ear shout, I don't know about my suggestion to letting our daughter go gallivanting with this young man, after the effect he had on her horse," Williams said.

"Which one do you worry about, that girl has nothing on her mind but that boy all the time," Kathy replied.

"I, well they're getting to that age ma, and we weren't any older than they are," he reminded her.

"I'm well aware of that, I just hope she'd wait till she got older than when we were married," Catherine replied.

"She may have if you hadn't made her so pretty," Williams said.

"Me?" She said, adding "you had something to do with that also."

"No she got her looks from you," Williams stated.

"Maybe but you were there also," she accused, "it's just that she'll be running off and getting married before we know it."

"Likely," William agreed.

"I hope and he seems like a fine man, I don't want her to get a bum, "Catherine explained.

"Horses sure do take to him," William observed, "We saw that with our own eyes."

"That is true, I suppose that does add in his favor," Catherine said.

"I don't know what we could ask for more than she finds a man who loves her and takes good care of her, respecting her," William began, adding "we should be happy for her however hard it is."

"I know I and I am, it's just hard," Catherine replied, he took her in his arms and gently hugged her.

Kyle and Lillie near to the hill by this time, they were talking about different animals they had seen here in the mountains, Lillie's father had come over here fifteen years before his parents had, he was fortunate to have an older man take him in and help him get started with the stock shortly after he and Catherine had got married, were his dad had started working in the mines, Lillie helped her dad she helped what's the cows and moving them if they were staying in one spot too long, they like to eat the young grass, it must have a better taste, she did this so her brothers could spend their time cutting and stacking hay, though in the wintertime her brothers fed the hay to them.

Kyle told her he worked with the horses most of the time getting them ready to race and breaking the younger ones, he said he liked to think of it as coaching.

"You sound like you know what you're doing, after winning five of eight races,"

Lillie praised.

"I have been fortunate to have a good trainer in Buck, that and we have Max and his offspring from your dad's stock," Kyle replied.

"Does he or is he that much faster," Lillie asked?

"Yes, see most horses win a race by a nose or a linked, he just runs away from them," Kyle explained, "does your dad ever race," he asked?

"No he just raises them and sell them to others," Lillie replied.

"He, you have good stock, we have four other two-year-olds out of Max that are not as fast but they are excellent riding stock," Kyle praised. "Buck has me to train all of the gentle riding ones he wouldn't be afraid to let his children ride, my brother Jim helps train also."

"You must be good if he lets you train the horses," Lillie speculated.

"Animals just seem to take to me is all," Kyle explained.

"I must be part animal," Lillie said.

"Why's that," Kyle asked?

"Because I take to you also," she explained.

"I see," Kyle said, "I never saw any animals that look half as good as you," he praised.

"Thank you," Lillie said, "there's a good spring down near our winter home if you're thirsty." She suggested.

"That sound like a good ideal, lead the way," Kyle replied, they slowly made their way to the house there was a ladle hanging by the pump, Lillie got it off the wire and held it under the spigot as Kyle pump it and she handed it to Kyle who took a drank.

"Now that is some good water," Kyle complemented her. They were standing close together facing each other and they leaned close together and kissed.

"Now that is definitely better than the water," Kyle said.

"Yes," Lillie agreed.

"We have to go slow," Kyle began but, Lillie cut him off with another kiss.

"But I don't want to," she explained.

"There are some things that have to wait," she cut him off with another kiss, this time it was a lot longer, "I know we can't wait very long till we get married," Lillie said.

"This time Kyle kissed her and it was even longer, this was the first kiss for both of them and has stirred emotions they didn't know they had, both of their hearts were racing and for a time they just held onto each other, a place that just felt right, after several minute they came apart.

"I better go or my mother will give me a hard time," Lillie said.

"Why," Kyle asked.

"I think it's, I am her oldest daughter and she's afraid you'll take me away," Lillie answered.

"Oh I guess that's true," Kyle agreed, "I definitely want you as part of my life," they came together for one lingering last kiss.

Lillie broke away and went to her horse, "I have to go before, Lord knows I don't want to," Lillie said, "bye,"

"I didn't; I know what you mean," Kyle said, "bye, I'll be back next Saturday if that's okay."

"It is very okay," Lillie smiled, she rode off, she turned and waved a few times till she went around the trees out of sight, Kyle mounted up after she went out of sight and started back to the ranch.

Lillie slowed down after she lost sight of Kyle because of trees, it was more what she wanted to do then to do with her mother though she was part of it, she'd never had feelings like this before, she was afraid and wanted to explode at the same time.

Kyle was thinking of her kiss and how he wanted more and will, more! Whose, whoa she's so wonderful! It may take some time to get his mind off Lillie but, he better get his mind on where he's going it was a long ride home and would be a longer one if he made a wrong turn, man until now he didn't come this way often, he needed to watch where he was going, yet what he wanted to do was turn around and go catch Lillie, though he knew she'd be home before he got there and that would be hard to explain so he kept going home.

Little did he know, Lillie was having similar thoughts of going after him, but she wouldn't let herself, this was a hard thing, she always had been able to do what her parents wanted her to do no matter what, but she had, well like her horse she just melted in his hands or arms and that was where she wanted to be. These were new emotions for both of them and they liked it, it was part of growing up.

Lillie got home and took care of her horse she rubbed her down real good before going to the house.

"He seems like a nice young man," Catherine said as she came in the door.

"Yes mother he is," Lillie agreed.

"That look well, it's like you're glowing with happiness," Catherine explored a little bit; "you'll be wanting to get married before we know it."

"There's no hiding anything from you," Lillie said.

"I was in your shoes not all that long ago and the love bug bit me and I melted into your Father's hands, I didn't want to leave and still don't," her mother explained, "I just ask that you don't hurry into anything."

"Mom I've never had these kind of feelings before," Lillie said.

"It doesn't get any easier till you do something about it and that makes it stronger," her mother explained.

"Stronger," Lillie asked?

"Not only will you want to know but, you will know and you will like it," Catherine explained.

"Oh," Lillie said, she was a little shocked and excited and scared altogether, shocked by what her mother was telling her excited by the wanting part, scared by not knowing what to do, was a lot to take in all in one day.

They were interrupted by her brothers coming home, so they didn't talk anymore, they went to fixing supper.

Later Kyle got back to Bucks ranch as he was rubbing down the mare Buck came to the barn.

"Hello Buck," Kyle greeted.

"Hello Kyle," Buck replied, "you have a nice ride?"

"Oh yeah!" Kyle answered.

"That's good?" Buck asked, "Did you mean your dad?"

"Yes I did, and he said twenty five dollars and the stud is Max's half-brother," Kyle explained, "he also said he'd give Max a race, not sure who would win, the feed may make a difference," he added.

"It's worth a shot for that," Buck said, "when she comes in, I'll have you take her back up there," Kyle smiled thinking to yourself that can be this week.

"How did your visit go?" Buck asked.

"Real well," Kyle answered, I got to meet Lillie's mother and dad, I got her dads permission to see her and they let her ride part of the way back to what they call their winter home," he explained.

"Lillie look some like her mother?" Buck asked.

"You'd think they were sisters, one looks just a little older than the other," Kyle answered.

"Now you see why my wife doesn't want me to go there, she thanks I look too long at her," Buck explained.

"Yes but your wife has nothing to worry about because you love her dearly," Kyle said.

"That is true," Buck agreed, "yet sometimes I'm at fault because I look longer than I should," he explained.

"I understand," Kyle said, "they are nice people, if anything at least they were to me, their straightforward, don't have to think about what they think, you're a lot like them."

"Why thank you Kyle, I appreciate that," Buck said, "one of the many things I like about you is your truthfulness, you and your brother Jim both."

"I apologize and if my head seems to be somewhere else, well it's just I've never had a girl strike me like Lillie has," Kyle explained.

"You'll get it lined out in time," Buck assured him, "and I do understand I was young not so long ago."

"You would think I was a blind man who could only see her," Kyle said. Buck laughed,

"That's how love works," Buck explained adding, there is nothing wrong with it.

"Except I'm here and she's not," Kyle said.

"I understand," Buck said.

"I better be heading home, I'll see you in the morning," Kyle said.

"Okay Kyle bye," Buck said, "oh be patient Kyle it gets easier."

"The patient part is the hard part." Kyle replied.

"True," Buck laughed. "True." With that Kyle headed home.

A very hard part of life Buck was thanking as he finished the day's chores, still a child but on his way to growing up, yes he remembered them and how he had felted after he had met his wife then the light came on, it has dimmed a little but doesn't go out, and yes when he was young he was blind like Kyle is now, in time Kyle's will be manageable with marriage and what comes after and hopefully the love will grow as his has with his wife, his thoughts were interrupted by his wife opening the door telling him supper was ready, he went to the pump and washed up for supper.

CHAPTER 4

Kyle was almost home by this time and Peter was on guard watching for him, he wanted to know if he was going to bring her home and he was disappointed when Kyle came home along.

"Where's Lillie at," was Peter's first question?

"She's at home," Kyle answered.

"Aren't you going to bring her home? Peter asked.

"You don't get to bring them home that soon Peter," Kyle replied."

"How come," Peter asked?

"It may take a little bit longer before you get to bring someone home," Kyle answered, "first you have to get to know each other, before you know if you want to marry," he explained.

"Don't you like her?" Peter asked.

"Yes," Kyle answered.

"Don't she like you?" Peter asked.

"Yes but, you have to get permission from our parents before you can marry," Kyle explained.

"Oh," Peter replied. "As you get older you will understand more," Kyle assured him.

"I hope so," Peter said, as he opened the door to the house, "Ma Kyle's home," he announced. "Just in time for supper," Barnabas said. Kyle was hungry but it wasn't for food.

"How was your afternoon?" Katie asked.

"It was good," said I got to meet Lillie mom and dad, their nice and they let her ride in little ways back with me."

"Does Lillie look like her mother," Katie asked?

"Yes," Kyle answered.

"I'm sure I've seen them in town," Katie said. "They are pretty."

"They are that," Kyle replied.

"He just have horses?" Barnabas asked.

"No they have quite a few cows too," Kyle answered.

"Must have a lot of land," Barnabas stated.

"I don't know how much land but, he has some in the flat land then some higher I didn't see all of it," Kyle said.

"Probably because your eyes were else where's," Jim teased.

"Jim," Katie exclaimed.

"It's all right mom, seeing as Jim has the same problem," Kyle replied.

"Buck's daughter," Barnabas Jr inquired?

"Yes," Kyle answered.

"I thought so," Barnabas Jr said.

"Yes we've seen the way you two look at each other at Church," Katie said.

"Does here parents know," Barnabas Jr asked?

"Oh yeah," Jim replied, "Her mother asked Becky about us."

"Barnabas it looks like we have two boys who are going to run off with some girls," Katie said.

"That we know of," Barnabas replied.

"What," Katie asked?

"I don't know of anything yet but, boys will be boys," Barnabas explained.

"True," Katie said.

"What does that mean," Peter asked?

"All boys get to a certain age, they get to thinking about girls," Katie explained, "and don't worry about it you've a ways to go."

"That's good," Peter said, "it seems like all they can think about is girls."

"Your days coming," Robert said.

"No way," Peter replied!

"Peter is running them all off with all of his questions," Alyssa stated and laughed, so did everyone else.

"You won't know anything if you don't ask," Peter said, "Pa said so."

Katie laughed, "Now we know! Now we know!" "Now we know what," Barnabas asked?

"Why Peter asked so many questions," Katie answered.

"I didn't know he'd be so inquisitive but, what I told him is true," Barnabas defended himself.

"I know I'm just funning you," Katie teased, "let's eat."

"What are we eating," Peter asked?

"Ham potatoes, gravy, and lettuce," Katie replied.

"Yum that sounds good," Peter said.

"I agree," Kyle said. They sat down and started filling their plates; it was quiet for a while as they were eating.

As was usual after supper the girls help their mother cleaning up the dishes, Barnabas went to read, Kyle went to wash off after his long ride.

Tomorrow would be a less hectic day though they would run some horses starting with close ones tried to find each one's fastest, how to set, were the best balance would be, Jim would be furthering his learning starting tomorrow, his next thought was Lillie, oh what tastes her kiss, yes he wanted to go back there, he would next weekend, but how he wish she was here now. His mind was strangely between the horses and Lillie, the Wild West it got stuck way back in a corner somewhere almost forgotten, he was thinking of the house for him and Lillie to live in and go from there.

She was so beautiful he hoped he could get his mind on the horses tomorrow and do his job right, it was getting hard.

Jim and Barnabas Jr were sitting outside enjoying the nice evening.

"What was he talking about," Jim asked?

"He saw me talking to Sally Ray the other day is all," Barnabas Jr replied.

"Y'all were friends in school," Jim pointed out.

"And we still are, and there is nothing past that," Barnabas Jr assured him.

"That's too bad, she's right pretty," Jim replied.

"There is no need to get in a hurry," Barnabas Jr explained.

"As long as no one else is," Jim replied, "say what happened to Paul Norman, I thought he was sweet on her?"

"They moved away last month," Barnabas Jr answered.

"Oh," Jim said, "just a thought." It also made Barnabas think that maybe he should talk a little more to Sally to see what her plans were, Kyle came back to the house after he was cleaned up breaking into Barnabas Jr thoughts, Kyle was ready to go to bed they started their day out early.

"Well good night; I'm gone to turn in," Kyle said.

"Good night," they both said in return, these three young men were having growing pains; Barnabas Jr and Jim got up and followed Kyle to bed.

As they were going to bed Katie was smiling, "what are you smiling about," Barnabas asks?

"Our boys are a lot like you," Katie answered, "one thing on her mind."

"I could think of two things at once," Barnabas argued.

"Yeah what," Katie asked?

"Getting home from work and you," Barnabas replied.

"I think that's just one," Katie replied.

"No you have to watch where you're going as your coming home," Barnabas argued.

"I see adding, let's just say you have a few things on your mind that there is one you keep there all the time," she explained.

"Well yeah," Barnabas said, "don't you?"

"It's there a lot," Katie answered.

They followed suit behind Kyle they when to bed; it was quiet for a while, though it was a little time before they want sleep.

Jim statement was keeping Barnabas Jr up thinking about Sally, truth he had thought about Sally but not seriously he was young and there was time but, what if she was the one, he thought I have to go to sleep; this is Kyle's fault he started this in the first place, and if I don't go to sleep I won't want to get up in the morning, I wonder if Kyle is having the same problem? He didn't know it did but yes Kyle was thinking about kissing Lillie and the emotion that it stirred inside of him, sometime later they both drifted off to sleep, it was about the same time that Lillie succumbed to sleep.

To the boys it seem like they had just gone to sleep when they hard their mother starting the stove for breakfasts; they all got up slowly dressed for the day and made their way to the table for breakfasts, their dad was smiling when they came in.

"Y'all go to sleep last night," he asked?

"Yeah," they answered.

"You look like you're still asleep," Barnabas said, "don't you think mother?"

Katie took a closer look, "yes, they must have something heavy on their minds," Katie observed."

"That or dreaming," Barnabas suggested.

"Perhaps it keeps waking them up," Katie added.

Barnabas was chuckling, "don't worry it gets better in time though it may get worse first," Barnabas assured them.

"Did you have problems like this when you were young," Barnabas Jr asked?

"Still do," Barnabas ameted, "if you're in love you will to."

"Hope I don't wake up like this every morning," Barnabas Jr stated.

"You won't, after a while seems like your body balances the sleep and dreaming the best I can describe it," Barnabas explained.

"I hope you're right," Jim stated. It wasn't long Katie was setting breakfasts on the table.

"Eat up boy's, help you make it through the day," their mother stated, "Bet you never thought girls would be such hard work did you," She ask?

"No," Barnabas Jr replied.

Barnabas and Katie laughed at his replied, they all ate their breakfast and said goodbye as they were leaving.

"Don't worry honey, we made it they'll make it to," Barnabas assured her.

"Oh I know," Katie replied, "I was wondering if we made our parents laughed like we are," she asked?

"I'm sure they did," Barnabas chuckled, kissed her goodbye, "I'll see you tonight honey."

"See you tonight," Katie replied, "be careful."

It was one thing to have Peter who asked so many questions it get your mind thinking but, on top of him she now had three love struck boys, Katie laughed, she was happy for them.

The boys were waking up from the walk, when they got to the turnoff they waited for their dad to catch up, "you boys try to stay awake today," Barnabas teased.

"We will," Kyle answered, "Y'all stay out from under the coal."

"That we plan to do," Barnabas said.

"See y'all this evening," Barnabas Jr said.

"Goodbye," the rest replied, with that said they all headed to work, upon arriving at the ranch they meet Buck coming out of the house.

"Good morning boys," Buck greeted, "How are y'all doing today," he asked?

"Were doing okay," Kyle answered.

"The Sunday ride more than he can handle Jim," Buck teased?

"I think it tested him," Jim replied.

"I'm fine." Kyle assured him, "what's on your mind this morning?" Kyle asked to change the subject.

"I thought we'd, or you two will start working with the yearlings," Buck answered.

"Okay," Kyle replied.

"You're learning and teaching, learning the youngsters and teaching Jim how not to get hurt," Buck explained.

"Okay," Kyle chuckled, "that'll depend on how good he can hang on," he suggested.

"We'll see if he has that calming touch like you have," Buck said.

"The touch," Jim asked? "Yeah, you see at best they only half-heartedly buck when he gets on them," Buck explained.

"He does have a way with horses I've seen," Jim agreed, "we'll see," Kyle and Jim tended to the morning feeding and then when to the pasture where the weaned horses were at, Kyle went out in the pasture to the gate to the lot, he opened the gate and when in all the horses followed him in, Jim came up behind them and close the gate, Jimwas thinking that they may have followed him in if he'd had a bucket of feed, but with Kyle they walked right to him to be petted.

"Let's start with a little grain and put a little hay in the rack as a treat, why don't you get the hay and grain," Kyle directed, "and I'll fill their water tank." After both of their appointed chores were done they went to the barn and got a couple ropes and a couple halters and reins and some lead rope.

"Today will start with those who let us put a bit in their mouth and then go to those who won't," Kyle said. Kyle had worked with them some but not a lot. Buck had two other their hands who worked at putting up hay, oats and corn, they mostly took care of the cattle and watched over the horses in the pasture's, and those in the higher pastures.

Kyle and Jim did the training and feeding for those closer to the house, a lot of trainers when about it by strength, Kyle's strength was his calm, the horses liked him and trusted him. Jim couldn't get over how the horses followed Kyle yes, they were tame, but still. Kyle put a bit in two horse's mouths and handed one to Jim, "talk to him in a calm voice and don't jerk on the reins, he'll follow you, he's been trained a little bit," Kyle instructed. This is how their day went.

Buck came by a few times, liked what he was seeing, Jim was doing well, not as smooth as Kyle was but all right, Kyle was good and what Buck really liked was he didn't let it go to his head, but a lot of people after last Saturday would have celebrated, Kyle took care of the horses and wonder what he could have done to do better, he was sure glad Barnabas and Katie came here from Ireland and started a family.

He went by again at three in the afternoon, "how is it going boys," Buck asked?

"So far there working well; we'll see when we tried to ride them," Kyle answered. "Good, let's put them out in their pasture and start the evening feeding and watering," Buck suggested.

"Okay will be along shortly," Kyle replied, Buck headed to the barns, Kyle and Jim slipped the harnesses and bridles off the horses and let them out into the pasture, shutting the gate behind them they went by the tack shed and put their tack up, Kyle started watering in the barns and Jim went to help Buck with the feeding.

"Well what do you think so far," Buck asked?

"There are three that stand out, they are built like Max, one of them is Max Junior's brother, there are others who will give them a run they just don't have the outward showing muscles," Kyle answered.

I kind of thought that to," Buck agreed, "I've watched them running out in the pasture there is a five or six ahead out in front of the rest it's like two groups," He explained.

"We'll see after we have a few days of riding them," Kyle replied.

"And see how they set," Jim added.

"See I told you, you would learn Jim and you are," Buck said.

"Still it is hard to remember everything," Jim replied.

"It gets easier with time," Buck assured him.

"The things you tried to remember will become second nature in time," Kyle explained, "when you get caught on to it, there is like a check list in your mind to look at the things you see to do and what works and what doesn't."

"Do you understand what Kyle means," Buck asked?

"I think so," Jim replied, "like if you get in the saddle and it feels like the saddles got a bump in the front, you know it's too far forward," he explained.

"That's right," Buck said, "the little things that you encounter and take care of may make the difference of winning or losing a race," he pointed out.

"I see what you mean," Jim said.

"Good, we better get to work Jim or we'll miss supper," Kyle stated.

"Don't want to do that, we may be like the horses and not do well tomorrow," Jim replied.

"See how life is like school we can find things that applied to our lives that can applied to animals," Buck said adding, "you don't eat you don't do good."

"True," Jim agreed.

They finished feeding and went home, their week went well, with good headway on the training, on Friday afternoon Buck was watching them, he was amazed at no harder they bucked while they were on them, Jim was on one of Max's daughters and yes he was getting a ride but, it was more like hopping not bucking, ever since Kyle started training his horses they didn't put up as much of a fight and in just weeks a child could ride them, to say the least Buck was very pleased.

"What do you think," Kyle asked?

"I'm very pleased with the way you were teaching your brother to train the horses," Buck replied.

"He is doing well," Kyle agreed.

"Kyle you have a way with horses I've not seen before, I'm lucky to have you," Buck praise.

"Ah; you trained me," Kyle stated.

"I did very little, you, Kyle you become their friend and it's like they're happy to see you," Buck explained, "and I don't have that gift."

"They think I'm going to feed them is all," Kyle stated to downplay the praise that Buck was given him; he didn't think he was anything special.

"You plan on going to see that young lady tomorrow," Buck asked?

"Yes sir if it's all right to borrow a horse," Kyle replied.

"That will be fine and while you're going take the red mare with you, she's in," Buck answered.

"Oh! I can do that," Kyle replied.

"I thought you might," Buck said smiling.

"I'll go up there after feeding in the morning," Kyle said.

"That will work," Buck replied.

"Next week are we going to run the race horses some," Kyle asked?

"Yes, a little," Buck answered, "I'll get the jockeys here Wednesday and will start and go as needed from there."

"Okay that sounds good," Kyle replied.

"Take your time with the young ones you've plenty," Buck said.

"We will," Kyle said, "I let them pick the pace, I just had to slow Jim down is all."

"He'll get it in time," Buck assured him.

"He's doing a good job he just pushes a little harder than I like to," Kyle explained.

"We'll work with him," Buck said, "I see he can stay in the saddle all right."

"Yeah, he got thrown this morning, landing on his shoulder and head, it about knotted him out but, he's all right," Kyle explained.

"He'll have to learn how to roll," Buck stated.

"That's what I told him," Kyle said.

"Look at that she's already quit, I can't believe it," Buck said, "I've never had horses this easy to break."

"You do now," Kyle replied.

"Yes I guess I do," Buck said, "maybe it's I'm not riding them," he suggested. They watched Jim rides the mare around the pin, she was tossing her head but, she didn't buck anymore, Jim was grinning from ear to ear, a young still boy getting to show off in front of his boss who was his girlfriend's dad to boot; this was good he thought, it was a good week but, landing on his head, his neck was a little sore was all.

The mare could feel his excitement she started to hop again causing Jim to quit daydreaming and pay attention to riding, after a few hops she stopped and Jim patted her neck talking to her to calm her down, the combination of both worked, he got off and led her toward Buck and Kyle, she followed him like she'd been doing it for a long time.

"Max must have rubbed off on her, he was like that too," Buck said.

"What do you think Jim," Buck asked."

"They're coming a long," Jim replied.

"We'll keep some of these to breed, depending on how they run and they're built," Buck said.

"How come she spooked," Kyle asked?

"I was daydreaming," Jim admitted.

"Oh, the next time roll when you're thrown," Buck advised.

"Yeah, I think it would save me some pain like I have now," Jim agreed.

"It took me a while to learn, I wasn't very limber and half the time I didn't land very good," Buck explained.

"Kyle told me to roll either sideways or like stick my head between my knees but, I didn't react fast enough," Jim replied.

"You'll get the hang of it with practice," Kyle assured him.

"I don't know about that the way no more than these buck," Buck said.

"There'll be some that won't be as easy as these," Kyle predicted.

"I'm sure you're right," Buck agreed. "Jim in the morning after feeding you get Max Jr and ride him about an hour, but too fast I just want to keep him loose, all those muscles he's got," He instructed.

"Okay I can do that," Jim answered.

"And then you get a couple of the older mares and you take Becky up on the upper meadows and make sure you look at the horses some," Buck teased.

"I will," smiling from ear to ear Jim answered.

"I know you will," Buck replied, "I was young like you two once and I know some things distract us."

"That can happen in your thoughts without the lady being with us," Jim said.

"True," Buck agreed, "as we get older it gets some easier."

"I hope so," Jim agreed, Kyle and Buck laughed.

"Well we better turn these out and start the evening feeding shortly," Buck suggested.

"Yes it's about that time," Kyle said, "Jim why don't you strip that mare and I'll start turning the other one's loose."

"That'll work," Jim replied.

"I'll go get some water running and meet you in the north barn," Buck said.

"Okay we'll be there shortly," Kyle answered. Buck went to the windmill and turned the water on, while Jim and Kyle turned the yearlings back to the pasture and they meet at the north barn.

"Kyle you start feeding them ready for racing and me and Jim will water," Buck instructed them.

"I can do that," Kyle replied, he started each with a gallon of oats but when they came to Max Jr he gave him a gallon and a half, he just took more than most to feed all those muscles, he did better on more grain than some of the others did, he'd found. Kyle finished feeding about the same time as they did their watering.

"Well how do they look to you," Buck asked?

"They look good," Kyle answered.

"But," Buck asked seeing the look on Kyle's face.

"I think we need to get started monday, at least walking them," Kyle replied.

"I trust your judgment," Buck replied, "so monday Jim you start walking them and by wednesday they'll be ready for the jockeys to start running them."

"I think that will help those that are close to better compete," Kyle explained.

"I agree," Buck said, "why don't we call it a day and get an early start in the morning," he added.

"Okay we'll see you in the morning, bye," Kyle replied.

"I'm going to tell Becky goodbye before I leave and I'll be home shortly," Jim said.

"Now how did I know that," Kyle smiled.

"Because you have the same desire to go see your young lady," Buck teased.

"Ain't that the truth," a smiling Kyle replied?

"Good night." They all laughed. "Good night, remember to sleep tonight don't dream it away," Buck advised.

"Okay," Jim replied, I'll be home shortly."

"All right I'll tell mom you be home later," Kyle said as he started for home, as he walked away the first thought excited him, tomorrow he would see Lillie before noon, all right! And he was still thinking about how warm Lillie's touch was when he came into the yard where Peter was waiting on him.

"Did you get bucked off?" were the first words out of Peter's mouth.

"No I didn't but, Jim did," Kyle replied.

"Bunches of times," Peter asked?

"No just once," Kyle answered.

"Did he not ride anymore," Peter asked?

"Oh yeah bunches of times," Kyle answered.

"Oh," Peter replied, he was disappointed.

Kyle change the subject on him, "did you get bucked off your horse today," Kyle asked?

"Yeah a few times," Peter answered.

"He must be a mean bronco," Kyle suggested.

"Yes he's fast to," Peter answered.

"Like Max," Kyle asked?

"Oh he's faster than Max," Peter replied.

"Man he must be fast," Kyle stated.

"He doesn't never lose," Peter replied. "That's good," Kyle replied.

"Yeah he's always way ahead of everyone else," Peter describes, "so when are you going to see that girl," he asked?

"Tomorrow," Kyle answered. "Oh, you must like her," Peter inquired.

"Yes I do someday you'll meet a young lady and you'll know she's the one for you, and you'll fall in love, and no it's not like loving mom and dad," Kyle explained. He got the, I don't understand look.

"You'll want to be with her all the time," Kyle stated. "You mean like with Billy," Peter asked?

"Yeah but different, when you get older you feel different about girls then you feel about boys," Kyle explained.

"If you say so," Peter replied, "but I ain't going to kiss no girl." Kyle laughed and was laughing when he went into the house.

"Well Peter must've struck your funny bone," Katie stated.

"Yes he did but, one of these days he's going to feel a lot different about girls," Kyle answered."

"Yes he will," she replied.

"I think I'll go get cleaned up," Kyle stated.

"Okay, I hope your father doesn't come back black today," Katie said.

"I hope so too," Kyle agreed, "someone is going to get hurt bad if they don't stop that falling coal from the ceilings and sides for that matter." That said Kyle got some clean clothes, a wash cloth and towel, he went out and put water in the tub and he replaced what he took and put a little wood in the stove to re-heat.

While he was cleaning up his sisters came in the house from the garden with fresh vegetables and started cleaning them for supper, they help their mother with the garden even the canning, Robert helped also he trapped rabbits, squirrels and fished, they also help dressed chickens and other wild birds they were able to shoot, then on tuesdays and saturdays their mother and the girls made fresh bread to keep it fresh, one of the boys milked the cow every morning and evening, the older boys dug potatoes and help weed the garden as needed, they all helped because they all liked to eat.

Kyle was drying off when his dad and Barnabas Jr walked in the yard they looked a lot clear today than they had for the last week.

"Didn't have any falls today," Kyle asked?

"No and it looks like were in better coal for a while," Barnabas Jr replied.

"That is good now maybe mother will worry less for a while," Kyle said.

"Let's hope so," his dad replied, "when we work steadily in the mine without any falls we can breathe some better."

"How about the wind," Kyle asked.

"It doesn't blow in the mines," Barnabas Jr replied.

"I was talking about the plant area," Kyle said.

"It can get pretty bad up there," his dad said. "How's the horse breaking going," he asked?

"These have been the best to break that I have ever worked so far," Kyle replied.

"How's Jim doing," Barnabas asked?

"Real good, he was only thrown once today," Kyle answered.

"How's he doing as a whole on the ranch," his dad asked?

"Real well," Kyle replied," Buck's been teaching him to decide what helps the horses to run faster," he added.

"Buck must see something in him," his dad stated.

"Yeah he does, the future son-in-law," Barnabas Jr stated.

"That is part of it," Kyle agreed, "but really he's learning fast."

"He sweet on Buck's daughter huh," their dad asked?

"Oh yeah"! Barnabas Jr confirmed.

"Hope he keeps his head on his job," Barnabas said.

"I think if anything it might be helping him," Kyle replied.

"Oh how's that," Barnabas asked?

"Well because Buck is Becky's dad Jim works real hard to please him," Kyle explained.

"That's good," Barnabas said, adding "working with your head somewhere else can get you hurt."

"That's the truth," Kyle said, "I put more water on to heat for y'all."

"Okay thanks, Barnabas you go first," his dad replied.

"Okay," Barnabas Jr said. While they were cleaning Kyle went out to the garden and helped his little brother he dug a few potatoes and a few radishes, he took them to the pump and cleaned them up and took them into his mother, she gave them to his sisters who peeled them and cut them up ready to put in the pan and put it on the stove, his sisters helped his mother a lot with the house,they also helped their mother clean other houses to, plus watching Peter which was a full-time job by its self, shortly after they had supper going Jim came home, after their dad got in the tub, Kyle refilled the kettle for Jim, not long after Jim finished his bath, their mother called them for supper. They had mashed potatoes, green beans, ham, lettuce, radishes, and green onions, and it was good.

"Oh mom this is good," Peter said.

"Yes dear as Peter says, this is good," Barnabas agreed, it was unanimous they all agreed.

"It's a pig," Peter observed, "where did Porky go to?"

"Oh he ran away," Katie said, Peter seem to be okay with Katie's answer, she didn't want to tell him he was eating him yet, she hoped he'd get a little older before he learned ham came from the pigs in their lot but, she didn't know about Peter, he asked so many questions.

"Boy these potatoes are good," Kyle said.

"So is the gravy," Jim added, to help get Peter's mind on something else.

"How's that radish Peter," Barnabas Jr asked?

"It is good and so were a green beans and onions," Peter answered. It wasn't long and supper was ate and the dishes cleaned and put away, and before they knew it the sun went down and they went to bed, during supper Peter got on how did vegetables grow, he knew that by eating you grow but what did the vegetables eat to grow?

Barnabas had tried to tell him about the nutrients in the ground but he didn't understand.

As they went to bed each of the older boys were thinking about their day, Kyle was thinking about tomorrow also and seeing Lillie, he was very happy that he would be going to see her, Jim is thinking about working the horses and how he going to take Becky for a ride up the hill, Barnabas Jr was just thinking about getting a girlfriend, he saw how his dad and mother loved each other and he wanted to feel that way also, he wanted it to be real like theirs was or is.

Kyle woke up at first light hearing his mother working with the cook stove getting the fire going, he dressed and went out to the woodshed and brought an armload to his mother.

"Oh, thank you," Katie said.

"You're welcome," he said as he grabbed a towel and wash rag on his way to the pump, he washed his face and hands preparing for breakfast.

When he came back inside Barnabas and Barnabas Jr were sitting at the table and he could hear Jim shut the door to the bedroom on his way to the kitchen, coffee was on and bacon was sizzling in the skillet, it wouldn't be long breakfast would be ready.

"Good morning," they all said.

"Y'all have a big day planned," Barnabas asked?

"I don't," Jim answered.

"I'm taking a mare up to Lillie's dad's place to have bred," Kyle replied.

"He mean going out to see his girlfriend and taking a horse while he's going," Barnabas Jr described.

"Maybe, works for me," Kyle answered.

"His mother laughed and said, "You mean a job you like."

"Yes," Kyle replied.

"You're truthful," Barnabas said.

"That's the way you taught us," Kyle replied.

Unless your truthfulness is to deliberately hurt someone," Barnabas stated.

"True," Katie agreed, "one of you boys set plates on the table, breakfast won't be long." They all got up and set the table, Barnabas Jr poured the coffee, Barnabas got the biscuits out of the oven and set them on a hot plate, Katie set bacon and eggs on the table and they all dug in, after Barnabas said grace.

Before they finished Peter came in and is first question was to Kyle, "are you going to marry Lillie?" his question caught Kyle off guard.

"I don't know," Kyle answered truthfully.

"Oh," Peter said, "don't you like her?"

"Yes very much," Kyle replied, "but what if she doesn't want to marry me," he asked?

"She does," Peter answered.

"How do you know that," Kyle asked?

"In my dreams I saw you and a girl getting married," Peter said.

"I see," Kyle said, "how do you know it was Lillie?"

"Someone said her name," he answered.

"Well you never know," Kyle said, thinking it was strange Peter dreamed about that. Peter asked a lot of questions.

"This was the first time he said he dreamed about anyone," Katie said to Barnabas as he was leaving to work.

"I thought that to," Barnabas agreed, "it may be just the first time he told us."

"That could be true, have a good day," Katie told him.

"I always have a good day when I come home to you," Barnabas replied. He gave her a kiss.

"She smiled, "love you," she said.

"I love you too," Barnabas said and gave her a big kiss before he left.

Kyle and Jim were already headed down there turnoff by the time Barnabas caught up to Barnabas Jr to go to the mine, by the time they got to the farm Buck was coming out of the house.

"Good morning boys how are y'all this morning," Buck greeted.

"Good," Kyle replied, "How are you?"

"Great," Buck answered, "let's get the feeding done and you can get on the road, Jim's going for a ride up the hill and I'll check everything here in the Valley while you're gone, take as long as you want, we'll feed tonight," he added.

"Thanks," Kyle replied.

"Don't give them too much time, Peter asked him this morning if he was going to get married," Jim said.

Buck laughed! "You never know Jim, that's kind of how it works, you meet the right one and you can't do without her," he explained.

"She's on my mind when I go to sleep and when I wake up," Kyle said.

"You've got it bad," Buck replied, adding, "Peter's probably right.

"Kyle's probably the only one who doesn't know it yet," Jim suggested.

"I wouldn't bet on that Jim," Buck said Kyle strikes me as one who knows where his heart is, given a little time he'll know for sure."

"I thought I didn't, I wanted to go to the wild of Texas till I caught a runaway horse with a redhead in the wild of Virginia," Kyle stated.

"The love of something or someone has a lot to do with shaping our lives," Buck said.

"I see what you mean," Jim said.

"He was going to work in the mine till he saw your daughter," Kyle explained.

"I kind of figured that and that's all right, she likes him and I'm sure he will do right by her," Buck replied.

"I guess if I'm going to go to Lillie's I better get started," Kyle said.

"I think he's telling us to quit stalling Jim, were holding him up from his gal," Buck replied. "I think so," Jim replied, Kyle just smiled went to the barn and started feeding.

"Kyle didn't feed the two he was taking a lot he had given them some extra hay yesterday evening it would stay with them for their long walk today, he did feed them a little grain first so they get done before they left, it was two hours before they finish.

"You think it might help Max junior's brother if I rode him today looking at the mares and cows Kyle," Buck asked?

"It definitely wouldn't hurt him that's for sure," Kyle replied, "that may be a good idea,"

I think I'll try it," Buck decided, we'll see you when you get back."

"Okay, I'd take Seven or Striker they didn't lose by that much," Kyle advised. "That's a good idea," Buck said, "Jim while you're getting the two mares that you and Becky are taking, bring me Seven.

"Okay I'll get them, be right back," Jim replied. Kyle went to get the two mares he intended to take they meet at the tack shed at the same time. "You go Kyle we're in no hurry," Jim stated.

"Okay thanks," Kyle replied, "you call this red mare Lightning, what are you going to call her colt?"

"We'll call it streak," Buck decided.

"That's a good name," Kyle said.

"Sounds like you have faith in the outcome," Jim stated.

"I do," Buck replied, "I believe she has the right bloodline to make the right mix," he explained.

"And we'll see in times," Kyle added.

"True," Jim agreed, Kyle finished saddling and mounted.

"I'll see you later today, bye," Kyle said.

"Like I said Kyle take your time," Buck reminded him.

"I will," Kyle replied and waved as he headed out.

"What do you think Jim about this young lady," Buck asked?

"I don't know her but she must be all right, and I think if she'll have him they'll marry," Jim answered.

Buck was curious for two reasons, one if Kyle got married he'd stay here, if not he would go to Texas, he was thinking how hard to push teaching Jim to learn from his brother about horses, he was pretty sure he would stay here, he didn't want to push either of them too hard, he was happy with both of their work and felt lucky to have them.

As Kyle left Becky came to the barn ready to go on a ride with Jim.

"Morning Becky," they said.

"Good morning, are we ready to go," she asked. Jim had just finished saddling the two mares as Buck was getting ready to mount Seven.

"Yes we're ready," Jim replied, they mounted and started there tour of the ranch.

Buck could feel the difference in the horse to the ones he normally rode; they just felt like a feeling of power under him, he didn't usually ride this caliber of horse because they didn't give as smooth as ride as these less muscle horses did.

He thought about Kyle's good eye to see the difference in horses, he said these were right up there with the top ones and after a short ride he believed him, he also thought that this would strengthen their muscles as he did, next week trial races would tell.

CHAPTER 5

Kyle was making good time today and not pushing the horses ether, he choose another mare to ride so Lighten wouldn't be so tired when she got there, he let them go at a faster walk eating up the miles.

His mother had made him a sandwich to eat on the way up to Lillie's which he did, it was a sunny warm morning though not too warm as it was at times, being in the mountains it varied, sometimes daily, it was getting to the hottest part of the year, he hoped they'd not be short of rain.

Buck had two workers who cut hay and worked on fence and the crops, it seem they worked on fence daily, horses where hard on fences, Buck looked at them two or three times a week, one had worked with the horses before Kyle took it over, which was okay with him, he didn't like getting bucked off the horses so it worked out.

Kyle had been thinking about work and he looked about and realized he was a lot closer than he thought so he decided to eat his sandwich and rest the horses for a bit but, not too long the horses seemed as eager as he was to get there, knowing the type of horses they were, Buck had a another line of breeding that he sold for riding stock they were a lot smoother, they were also what Buck rode most of the time.

Kyle thought Buck would be tired after riding the young racehorse today, tomorrow was a day of rest and after a few more minutes rest Kyle started off again, the mares were restless eager to be going, just a little bit further and he was where he first saw Lillie, not much further he came across her two brothers cutting hay, it was the first time they'd meet.

"Good morning," Kyle said.

"Good morning," they replied.

"I'm Kyle O'Reilly," he introduced his self.

"You're that fellow our sisters taken a shine to," her brother Ross stated."

"Sure hope you don't disappoint her," her brother Bo said, I'm Bo this is my brother Ross," he introduced.

"Pleased to meet you and I hope to honor your sister," Kyle stated, "the truth is I've never had a girlfriend before so I have things to learn."

"Don't we all," Ross replied.

"You just don't know about women, one day everything is great the next a man can't do anything right," Bo said.

"I guess that is part of our learning," Kyle said, "I've notice that between my folks and dad doesn't argue with her when she's like that.

"It's probably best," Ross said, "that the mare your boss wants breed," he asked?

"Yes," Kyle answered.

"My, she is a good-looking mare, they should throw a good colt," Ross replied.

"We're hoping so," Kyle stated.

"How come he doesn't breed her to Max," Bo asked?

"We have some of his colt's, my boss wanted to try a little different mix and your dad said Max has a half-brother as good or better than Max," Kyle explained.

"That's true, Rob I think is just a little faster than Max and they were just on grass," Ross agreed with his dad.

"Well I guess I'll go up to the other house," Kyle said, "is your dad there?"

"Yeah he brought Rob up yesterday, he thought you may show up today with a mare," Bo replied, "you know that mare looks an awful lot like Maxes mother."

"I thought that to," Ross agreed."

"You never know they could be kin," Kyle suggested.

"Could be," Ross replied, "go on up top dad is around there someplace." With a wave Kyle started towards their summer home, he liked what he saw in Lillie's brothers, they seem like real hard working young men.

"He went up the hill and looked out across the flat he could see some buildings and behind them he could see a small stream coming out of the mountain, he rode across the flat to the house, dismounted and knocked on the door, no one answered, the second time we heard a dog bark behind the house somewhere.

He remounted and rode around some trees then spotted them by a corral, Lillie and Catherine were watching William training a young horse, Lillie was the first to see him and she squealed, and came running, as Kyle got off his horse she ran into his arms and gave him the kiss.

"Lillie, how are you," Kyle asked smiling.

"I'm fine now that you are here," she answered, "how are you doing?"

"Great now that I'm with you," Kyle replied, she kissed him again.

"What will your mother and your dad say," Kyle asked?

"I told them we're getting married soon." Lillie informed him.

"Oh! Oh!" Kyle explained, "That's funny, my little brother Peter asked this morning if we were going to get married."

"Oh what did you tell him," Lillie asked?

"I didn't know I had to asked," Kyle's reply.

"I see," Lillie said.

"If I asked what will you say," Kyle asked?

"Are you asking," she asked?

"Yes," he answered.

"When do you want to get married," Lillie replied.

"Yesterday," he answered.

"Yes," Lillie said.

"I have to ask your mom and dad," Kyle said.

"They know," she said.

"Still have to ask its only right," Kyle stated.

"Okay," Lillie said and kissed him. They walked over to the fence where her mother and dad stood.

"Good morning," her mother said, Lillie says you to have something on your mind," Kyle was taken aback by this directness.

"Yes ma'am I would like your daughter's hand in marriage," Kyle asked.

"It is hard to give away our daughter, I asked that you wait a little while," Catherine stated?

"I know how you feel because I felt the same way when I met her mother, like she says we ask you wait a little while to make sure you love each other not the newness," William stated.

"Yes sir, we'll wait a while," Kyle assured them.

"Not too long, Lillie put in, while hugging Kyle."

"Boy you're in trouble, Catherine stated.

"You brought your bosses mare I see," her dad said.

"Yes where would you like her," Kyle asked?

"We'll put her over in the pin with Rob," Williams said, "I'll keep an eye on them to make sure they breed.

"Okay," Kyle replied, then he tied the horse he rode to the fence while Lillie held Lightning, then Lillie led her over to Rob's pin and after Kyle open the gate they took the lead rope off they turned her in, they started circling each other getting acquainted.

"I don't think there'll be any problem the way they're acting," Williams said.

"I think you're right," Kyle agreed.

"Sure looks a lot like Maxes mother," he said.

"That's what Ross and Bo said," Kyle replied.

"You meet our boy's," William asked?

"Yes," Kyle answered, adding, "They said the same thing about her and told me were you'd likely be."

"They didn't do anything mean did they," Lillie asked?

"Oh no, not at all," Kyle answered.

"They better not," Lillie stated.

"Your brothers are better than that," Catherine said.

"It's all right there were nice, and friendly," Kyle said.

"They better be," Lillie replied adding, "They're always doing something."

"No more than you do to them," her dad pointed out.

"Well, usually there are two against one," Lillie said.

"I know but, they're not that bad," William responded.

"How many is in your family," Kyle asked?

"Five," Lillie said, "How many did you say are in your family," she asked?

"Seven of us, five boys, two girls," Kyle answered.

"Your mother has a big family to care for," Catherine replied.

"True but, I think she would be okay with more, that's what she always tells us," Kyle said.

"I can understand that I think but, we don't get to decide everything," Catherine stated.

"True, I think God had pity on her after she had Peter, he can asked more questions than any ten people do," Kyle explained. "He keeps everyone thinking."

"A little boy about five," Lillie asked?

"Yes that's his age," Kyle answered.

"I think we've seen your mother," Lillie said.

"Oh I think you're right," Catherine agreed, "two girls a little order say seven and ten," she asked?

"Yes, mother thought she had seen you two in town," Kyle said, "She's tall like you two are." "Yes I know we have," Lillie replied, "I remember thinking your mother has a lot of patience, your little brother kept asking her question after question," she stated.

"He's like that most of the time but then, sometimes when he's thinking you wouldn't know he's there till he gets started again," Kyle described him.

"Ross is a little like that," her dad said, "what do you do for Buck, Kyle," he asked?

"I train horses, break some for riding, condition them the best I can for racing," Kyle answered, "we haven't any that are close to Max but one of his sons and maybe three of his one-year-olds may give him a race someday," he added.

"I'm glad he's working out for him, I don't care much for running the races myself," William said.

"It's part of my job the racing, but I like the training them the most," Kyle said.

"If you have the patience it's a good job and rewarding," William agreed.

"Each horse has its own personality, working with them is like figuring out a puzzle," Kyle explained.

"I agree with that, I've known some people who try to treat them all the same, it just makes the job harder," William agreed.

"True," Kyle said, "very true."

"And you can tell some people that and they'll never understand, no matter what you tell them it doesn't sink in, you have an insight some people never grasped," Williams said.

"I started working for Buck four years ago and he didn't criticize me when I started treating the horses differently than his other trainers were, two years ago he put me to training some of them, and he liked the outcome, last year he put me in charge of training," Kyle explained.

"What about the old trainers," Lillie asked?

"At first he was mad but, then he admitted the horses did respond better to me and he wasn't all that fond of being bucked off as he was getting older," Kyle replied, "Buck put him in charge of the crops, buildings and fences, called him the foreman."

"How do you two get along," William asks?

"There was some envy for a little while, then he admitted that the horses responded quicker and were tamer, that and I treated him respectable now we get along real good," Kyle answered.

"That's good," Lillie replied.

"Lillie while I'm working with these horses, why don't you take Kyle out and count the cattle," William suggested, "Oh make sure you see the red cow with just the white face see if she's had her calf yet," he added.

She looked to Kyle, who nodded his head, "okay we can do that," she replied, "Kyle we have to go get my mare."

"Lead the way," Kyle replied. They went to the lot next to the barn they went in and Kyle picked up her saddle and blanket, she picked up her bridal, she led the way into the lot shut the gate behind; her mare walked up to her and let her put the rains in her mouth and let Kyle put the blanket and saddle on, Lillie got on her and rode out the gate which Kyle opened for her, she rode to Kyle's horse and waited on him to mount.

"Lead the way," Kyle said, she led off and Kyle got to see some other beauty of Virginia besides Lillie, the hillside was about five hundred acres with a vast majority of it had grass covering it there were little valleys and hills all over.

"How many cows do y'all have," Kyle asked?

"Over two hundred," Lillie replied, "that's why my brothers cut hay all the time, plus we have forty horses," she added.

"Wow! And y'all take care them all by yourselves," Kyle ask.

"Yes," Lillie answered, "other than cutting and feeding hay they pretty much take care of themselves, we moved them back below after the first snow sometimes we wait 'till the second our third snow depending on how cold it gets," she explained.

"We feed grain to our racehorses, it helps them to be stronger and faster, there is not a whole lot of difference it varies with the horses," Kyle explained.

"How's that," Lillie asked?

"Well take Maxes Jr, he can eat a gallon more grain than any of the rests of them but, you have to give him a lot less hay or he doesn't run as fast," Kyle explained.

"How do you know that," she asked?

"Well we run them to get them in shape against each other and we tried different feedings to see what helps and what doesn't," he explained.

"Oh that makes sense," Lillie acknowledged, "my brothers Ross runs some around but they just get grass and hay."

"Looks of this grass I bet they do well at that and your cows look very good, full," Kyle praised.

"Thank you, dad thinks they do well on this grass I've heard him say, most everyone who buy our horses says they look good and full and like the way they ride," Lillie said.

"I remember when we got Max, just leading him to his stall I could feel the difference in his strength from ours," Kyle stated.

"I cried when dad sold Max, I love to ride him," Lillie omitted.

"I think I know how you feel when we sell one I've trained it's like a part of you is gone," Kyle said.

"That's what dad said when he sold Max," Lillie replied.

"They do become part of our lives," Kyle agreed.

"So when do you want to get married," Lillie changed the subject.

"Soon as I can get a place to move into," Kyle stated. "What about you?"

"Today, right now," Lillie replied with a big smile.

"I know what you mean, you're all I think of," Kyle said.

"I know, I was afraid you wouldn't come today and I don't know where you live but, I was going to find out today or tomorrow if you didn't come," Lillie explained.

"I didn't want to leave last week and I've wanted to come all week," Kyle stated.

"I wanted you here all week," Lillie said.

"Well soon we will be together all week, Kyle said with a big smile on his face.

"I know but, waiting is the hard part," she smiled.

"Yes so how many cows have you seen," Kyle asked?

"Fifty seven and same amount of calves," Lillie said, "you?"

"The same," Kyle answered.

"I didn't know you were counting," Lillie said.

"It's a habit, we have horses in different pins and I count them all the time," Kyle replied, "we have some in barns that we race, we walk them a lot, then the week before the race, we race them with another so they don't shy away," he explained.

"Does your boss have a lot of mares," Lillie asked?

"All total around fifty, we pick from thirty of them for racing and others are really good riding horses, he sales the colts out of them," Kyle explained, "he also sales some of what he calls his race line, he has already sold four of Maxes colts but, they didn't have the speed that Max Jr has, though there some faster than most," he added.

"How many do you have total," Lillie asked?

"Let's see we stay around one hundred fifty," Kyle answered.

"Do you and your brother take care of all of them," she asked?

"To a certain extent, we care for the racing horses and break the riding stock and help feed all of them in the wintertime, Buck has two sometimes three other hands who feed and cut hay, fix fence, barnes and things like that around the ranch, Kyle explained.

"Buck have a family," Lillie asked?

"He has two daughters, one a little younger than me and one six." Kyle answered.

"One close to your age," she asked?

"I would have to fight my brother for her but no, she doesn't appeal to me," Kyle stated, adding, "My heart belongs to you."

"I hope so," Lillie replied.

"Buck's daughter is like a sister to me, I don't think of her like I do you," Kyle explained.

"I'm just teasing you," Lillie replied "you feel the way about me as I do about you."

"You're the only one for me," Kyle inquired?

"Yes, because I feel you're the only one for me," Lillie answered. He leaned over and gave her a kiss, their horses moved and they about fell off, they laughed.

"I guess we should get on with our counting," Kyle suggested.

"Yes we should but, I do like those interruptions," Lillie replied with a smile.

"Me too," Kyle confessed, Lillie led off, they were gone three hours, her dad knew they would be which was fine, he wanted them to get to know each other past the newness.

"It's past that, she knows what she wants and that's him," Catherine stated.

"Be that what it may," William replied, "I want her to be sure."

"Oh she's very sure," Catherine said adding, just like we were when I met you."

"That's what I'm afraid of, as I recall we were so poor we couldn't buy anything," he pointed out.

"Oh we had something," Catherine corrected him, "each other."

"True," he agreed.

"And look at what we have made a family," she said, "we also knew there'd come a day we have to let her go."

"I know honey I just want her to be sure," he explained.

"I know and it doesn't make it easy to let her go," she replied, "sons normally don't go far but, one doesn't know about her daughter," she explained.

"True again," he replied, "since he's come into our life she's a different person."

"That was a reply my dad made about me when you came into my life," Catherine said.

"And I'm being like your dad," he asked?

"Yes somewhat," see answered.

"I remember saying I'm, or I'll not do that to my daughter, and I'm doing it," he'd knowledge.

"When we are young we don't think about tomorrow yet, when we are old we want our children to think about tomorrow so it won't be as hard for them," Catherine analyzed.

"What are you thinking then," William asked?

"That there comes a time when we have to let themgrow up," Catherine answered.

"You thank, now is that time for her," he asked? "Yes I do," she replied.

"He seemed like a good lad," Williams said.

"And if he hurts her, you'll put knots all over his head," she finished for him.

"Yeah," he replied.

Those are some good looking bulls y'all have, Bucks aren't near that big," Kyle said.

"They have grown a lot in five years dad's had them," Lillie replied, "I think dad called them Herford's," she added.

"Boy their big and your calves look good and strong to," Kyle comment.

"Thank you, my dad bought them, and it has made our calves more valuable when he sells them," Lillie said.

"I have to tell Buck that, our calves don't look near as big as these," Kyle answered.

"They really look that much better," Lillie asked.

"Yes," Kyle answered, "these are taller and thicker."

"Huh" how many cows do y'all have," Lillie asked.

"Forty angus, they're all black and short," Kyle explained, "they don't take much tending to, not like the horses."

"Yeah my dad works with our horses a lot," Lillie said, "one thing he did up here was run our spring through our lots save a lot of time," she added.

"Yes that helps a lot, we have pipes going to our lots from the windmill pump, that saves us a lot of time," Kyle explained.

"My mother makes sure nothing keeps water from going into each lot, it's her daily job," Lillie said.

"My mother cleaned houses some of the wealthy folks in town, it helps my dad make ends meet," Kyle said.

"I could do something like that," Lillie said, thinking of some way to help their living.

"We'll see if I can get that house that Buck has near where I live now there is a place for a big garden maybe you could sell vegetables from it," Kyle suggested.

"Maybe, we'll figure out something," she said, not that she was against raising a garden, she didn't know exactly what she wanted to do only she wanted to be in his arms, after that everything else would be okay.

Kyle was thinking he had some money so he would be able to buy the things that they need, he had been saving money to go west, and now that he had found all of the wild that he wanted, he could use that money to buy the things they needed for a home, oh not only was she wild she was beautiful. It was funny how we change our minds when we see what we really want, wow!

Lillie knew she wanted Kyle as soon as she saw him, and then the kiss! 'Oh my' she'd never felt like that, his touch just warmed her all over.

"They're all here I guess we can go home now," Lillie said, though she was in no hurry.

"Okay," Kyle replied as he reached out and touched her hand, "lead the way." Instead of going Lillie got off her horse, so Kyle followed her and she came into his arms and they kissed.

"Home can wait for a little while," she said and kissed him some more.

"I'm ok with that," Kyle replied when they came up for air. They kissed again for a lot longer time, she lay against him for a long time after, she's so warm and her hair smelled go good, Kyle was thinking, her being in his arms felt well, just right, like she belonged amongst other things.

She looked up and smiled and kissed him again, after what seemed a short time they came apart.

"I guess we better get home, though I don't want to," Lillie said.

"Yeah I suppose we should go, your dad will be wandering about us," Kyle said.

"He's a normal dad who loves his daughter," Lillie replied.

"That makes him a good dad," Kyle added, "he wants you to make good decisions, I can understand that, if I had a daughter I wouldn't want her to go after just anyone."

"But I'm not after just anyone," Lillie pointed out. "True, he just wants you to be sure, because when we marry it's for life," Kyle explained.

"It is and we will be happy for life, I just know we will," Lillie said, I felt that way since I first laid eyes on you, that's when I fell in love with you," she added.

Kyle smiled and said, "The same day I fell for you and the love grows every time I see you."

"I feel the same way," Lillie proclaimed.

"We'll marry soon as I get us a home," Kyle assured her. Lillie smiled and led off back toward the house. All of Kyle's dreams of adventure were put on hold, he never dreamed what a kiss could do to a young man, his thoughts of riding a horse all over Texas had vanished, all he wanted is here in Virginia and he can hardly wait.

Lillie had never been kiss nor did she dream a kiss would taste so good, it was like sweet but not like sugar, it was better.

They were thinking of what came next when they came into the yard one look was all her mother needed.

"Well Hun we can say goodbye to our daughter, that boy couldn't get away from her on our fastest horse," Catherine said.

"I've seen that look before on you," William replied, "lucky man."

"Yes I think we taught our daughter the things she needs in life," she agreed.

"He must be trustworthy when Buck lets him train his horses," Williams surmised.

"That is true," Catherine agreed, "as yet you haven't let our boys did a lot of that."

"I have been thinking about that, and yes I need to train the boys on how to train horses he agreed," Kyle and our boys are about the same age and yes I thought they were a bit young," he added.

"I can understand her thinking," Catherine agreed, "I hope they'll learn to be patient, by watching you I can see you have to be patient." She knows the boys had watched their dad work with horses and seen him use a strong but steady hand, and she had saw they were still rough.

"Perhaps I haven't used patient training on the boys like I have used on the horses," William acknowledged, "but they are young and rash in my tolerance for them is less than my tolerance for the horses perhaps we both have learning to do."

"Yes and they will," Catherine encouraged him, "take your time dear."

"I guess she sees something we don't," William acknowledged.

"We use our eyes, she uses her heart which looks deeper than the eyes," Catherine explained.

"And many times is shared," William replied. Lillie and Kyle walked up from the barn; they put her mare in her own pen and Kyle's in one of the empty ones.

"We saw all of them dad," Lillie said.

"That's good her dad said, "thank you."

"We both came up with same number," Lillie said, "I didn't know he was counting till he asked me how many I had and I told him, and he said that was what he came up with to," she added.

"Its second nature I'm always counting the horses in the different lots and pastures for Buck, his cow's to," Kyle explained.

"I understand it gets to be a habit after you do it a lot," William agreed, "so you train Bucks racehorses," he asked?

"Yes and I also trained the riding stock that he sales," Kyle answered.

"Does he have other trainers," Catherine asked?

"Actually I'm training my younger brother how to train them," Kyle replied.

"Is that the one who's sweet on your bosses' daughter," Lillie asked?

"Yes," Kyle answered, "he had asked Buck's permission for me to teach him and Buck agreed." He explained.

"How is he doing," William asked?

"He's learning," Kyle replied.

"Buck must think a lot of you to let you train his horses and your brother," Catherine said.

"I think he is pleased with the results we've been having so far," Kyle answered.

"And his daughter," Catherine asked.

"She's like a sister, I've been there for four years and no I've never thought of her like I do Lillie, Becky and my brother hit it off right away," Kyle explained.

"I think I understand that, I never felt for anyone else the way I feel for my wife, and Lillie is like her mother in her eyes you're hers and no one else can touch you or the flight will be on, that is the way Catherine is" Williams described his relationship with Catherine.

"She has no worry, there is definitely no one else," Kyle assured them.

"That's good, you see her mother has a cast iron skillet," he began.

"I only used that once," Catherine interrupted.

We have rubbed his head and said, "I still haven't notch in my skull," and laughed.

"I fell in love with Lillie at first sight, no one has ever moved to me in such a way, I go to bed with her on my mind and she's there when I wake up and stays there," Kyle explained.

"It's the same with me," Lillie replied, "no matter what I'm doing you're there."

"I know that's right, on the way home after she met you, she rode right by the road that comes up here," Williams said.

"Oh dad," Lillie replied.

He laughed, "it doesn't change with age and I think about her mother all the time," her dad explained.

"It's the same for me, even when I used the rule of iron," Catherine replied, "I didn't want to get rid of him just get his attention was all, she explained.

"You did that," William assured her; that is after I woke up."

"I didn't knock you out," Catherine corrected him.

"That's true but, I still woke up he explained, "I wasn't considering anyone else and looking back I can see what you thought you were seeing."

"That Becky Johnson was being too fresh," she explained.

"Oh dad, Lillie exclaimed! "Becky?"

"She never turned my head I was just being polite," he explained.

"To polite, her mother replied adding, "Becky wasn't always such a large woman, when she was young she turned a lot of eyes her way."

"No way," Lillie asked?

"Yes way but, with each child she kept what she gained," Catherine explained.

"Getting what," Lillie asked?

"Weigh, she got bigger with each child," her dad explained.

"And after ten she's big," Catherine added.

"I can't imagine Becky ever been small," Lillie said.

"She was and she tried to get every man around, married or not and then Paul caught her," Catherine explained.

"Way more woman than he knew," her dad said and laughed

"She is five feet two inches tall and weighed two hundred pounds," Lillie described.

"That must be Paul's mother," Kyle said adding, "He helps at the races."

"Yes they have a son named Paul, he's next to Luke and then Becky Mae," Catherine named them.

"Be careful Kyle she'll be getting her mother's rule of iron," William teased.

"I'll definitely keep that in mind," Kyle replied, "though she has no need of it."

"That's good," Lillie smiled.

"Lillie you should go cook some lunch and show Kyle you can cook," her dad suggested.

"Yes I'll help you dear so you aren't distracted and burn it," her mother offered.

"I won't be," Lillie stated, Lillie and her mother headed to the house to cook their meal, Catherine had gathered some vegetables out of the garden earlier in the day her dad had dug some potatoes, some of the green beans she had gathered and washed were on the rack of the outdoor cook stove simmering, while Lillie and Kyle were checking the cattle.

Her dead killed two squirrels and a rabbit which he had skinned and put in a sack to soak in the Creek, he had built a cage to keep the dogs and cats out of them, hunting animals and fishing in the stream was a part of their lives, larger game like deer in the warmer weather that made jerky out of it so it would last, their boys ate a lot of the jerky, so hunting and fishing didn't keep them from the field. Chickens and other wild birds and canned goods were also on their diet, they did eat well and very little of it came from a store, this wasn't because of the vicinity of the store, for even town people grow most of their own food and canned it, also keeping back seed to plant the next year, they had to keep it in a sealed can to keep varmints out of it, most everybody had a coonhound or more to help keep raccoons and such animals out of their gardens because they would destroy them, everyone kept their gardens clean for the best results of growth, and everyone had some kind of fruit trees, most everyone had apple and peach trees, and in the winter on cold days they cracked pecans and walnuts and picked those out after their feeding, most had hay in barnes or fenced in areas near water, putting up hay was a long hot job in the summertime, after hay time they cut the winter supply wood.

Lillie's family also tanned hides of the wildlife they killed and the cowhide when they butchered, they also saved the feathers from the chickens to make their beds and pillows softer and they sold some of them to the stores who resold them.

They had fenced areas in the lower part where they raised wheat and corn most was for feeding the stock but some was made into flour and cornmeal, they keep a few hogs in the higher barn lot there was usually a few up there running loose those were usually small, they didn't take them below till after the corn was harvested.

"Kyle helped Lillie's dad clean weeds out of the garden while waiting for the dinner; they talked about horses and cows and different plants as they worked.

Lillie wouldn't let her mother helped cook, so she cleaned close by keeping her eye on the meal, normally she wouldn't worry, because numerous times Lillie had made the meal without any help from her, she just wanted to make sure she didn't get distracted. Lillie had her mind on her job, she too wanted to do a good job, and they didn't know Kyle wasn't hard to please.

"This is delicious," Kyle praised, "Lillie this taste good,"

"Lillie cooked all of it but the green beans, so good or bad she gets the credit she wouldn't let me help," Catherine announced.

"It is very good," Kyle said before taking another bite of squirrel, Lillie was smiling and very happy for the praise of her cooking, she wanted to earn his praise not get false praise because she's a good shaped woman.

Kyle was thinking a beautiful woman, one who can cook to, what more could anyone want, the way he had seen his dad look at his mother now he understood why, he saw the same look on Lillie's dads when he looked at Lillie's mother, it was the look of true love, he was learning more about the difference of love.

A mother's love for a child is for protecting, a child loves a parent as a guide, a hand to lead, but this love is a partnership you each become part of the other, it just hit him, she's with him everywhere he goes and to lose her would be losing part of his self.

After the meal was finished, William said, "Come on Kyle now we are in the way, let's try your hand out on a stubborn colt I have over here in another pin.

"Okay, thank you Lillie the meal was delicious," Kyle praise.

"You're welcome," Lillie replied, "good luck," the colt her dad was working with was wild and stubborn.

Kyle wasn't worried though he'd worked with wild before, they went around the barn to a corral on the other side and as they approached the colt ran nervously to the other side.

"This one has been skittish all her life," William informed him and he took the rope off the gate.

"Wait just a minute with the rope and let me go it alone if you don't mind?" Kyle said.

"Okay want me to back off a ways," William asked?

"If you don't mind," Kyle replied.

"I don't mind," William answered he walked over and around the edges of bran and peaked around to see Kyle work, Kyle went into the lot and slowly walked across the lot to the other side not paying any attention to the colt, Kyle was whistling very softly and was alone and the colt walked toward Kyle, Kyle acted like he didn't see him he started walking away and the colt followed, stopping and starting a few times finally turned touched the colt and the colt runoff a little ways, Kyle continuing to whistle started slowly walking away again and the colt came back and this time let Kyle touch him before he ran away, but he came back they did this five times and finally he didn't run off, he went over to the gate and the colt followed him, Kyle picked up a halter and slowly put it on him he ran off and shook his head and after a few moments came back, all of this time Kyle was whistling very softly, Kyle had a rope in his hand and he tied the rope on, whistling and walking slowly the colt put slack in the line and stayed with him.

Kyle motion for William to come over and he did and when he came into the lot the colt shied away from him, he didn't like it. "Whistle softly," Kyle instructed him, he did and after a few minutes he stopped fighting the rope.

Catherine and Lillie came out as William was leading the colt.

"Well I never," Catherine whispered.

William brought him over to the gate and he shied away till he heard Kyle's soft voice it calmed him and he perked his ears up.

"How did you do that dad," Lillie asked?

"I did," he replied, "I didn't do anything and if I hadn't seen it I'd not believe it either," he added.

"How," Catherine asked?

"He went out there in the lot and started walking around like he was looking for something and softly whistling and the colt started following him like he was his mother," William explained.

"Oh," Lillie questioned.

"Well you're no different than the colt," William said.

"Oh dad," Lillie exclaimed.

"Tell me you're not ready to follow him home," William challenged her.

"I can't," Lillie started, "yes dad I would go with him right now," adding, "but he says we have to be married with yours and mom blessing."

"William, I'm liking this young man more and more each time we see him," Catherine said.

"I am to and I'm of a mind to go talk to Buck see if he'll let our boys come over this fall and have Kyle teach them some about training riding stock," William stated.

"He might," Kyle replied, "I know he has some young mares he'd like to get some different blood in," He suggested.

"Oh," William inquired.

"He'd pay for that I'm sure," Kyle stated.

"We could maybe trade some training for stud fee," Williams said, "you ask him about it and I'll go by and talk to him sometime in a few weeks, I can see there's going to be a wedding soon."

"Yes sir with you and Lillie's mother's permission and when I get us a house to live in," Kyle asked.

"You have our permission and I know if I said no she'd run away anyway, and anyone that can win the trust of this wild colt like you did this one is trustworthy, animals don't trust just anybody," William explained.

"I agree," Catherine added.

"Do you mean it dad," Lillie asked?

"Yes," William answered, she gave her dad a big hug and the colt got a little closer to Kyle.

"See what I mean," Williams pointed at the colt adding, there are few people that get that kind trusts out of any animal," he stated, "I've seen it with people who have animals a long time but, not to strangers."

"There's just something about my voice," Kyle said downplaying his ability. "There's that but, there is more," Williams said, "now I understand why Buck trust you so much."

"Why is that," Lillie asked?

"Lillie what did your mare do when Kyle went with you in the lot," Catherine asked?

"She came right to us," Lillie replied.

"What does she do if your brothers go in to saddle her," Catherine asked?

"She runs away from them," Lillie answered.

"She even runs from me," her dad replied.

"Not every animal takes to me like horses," Kyle stated adding, "Buck's cows don't follow me like horses unless I have a bucket of corn, and no other girl has drawing so much attention to me and in my mind all the time, when we're not together your always on my mind, it's like you're with me wherever I go."

"I know what you mean," Lillie said, "I think of you when I wake and I'm thinking of you when I go to sleep and all the times in between," she explained.

"My boss told me I'll think about what you'll think about decisions I make," Kyle said.

"That is when you truly fall in love," William said.

"Oh how do you know that," Lillie asked?

"Very shortly after I saw your mother that is how I started thinking," William replied, "it was no longer I, it was we."

"What will she be okay with or what will make her happy," Kyle added.

"That's love at the fullest," William said, Lillie smiled and brightened, every little doubt gone.

"I have to go look in on the other kids," Catherine said, "come on Lillie you'll have him all to yourself soon and leave your poor old mother to care for the house along," she added.

"It won't be long and you have more help mother," Lillie pointed out to her."

"I know, I'm just teasing you," she replied.

"Mother," Lillie exclaimed! They all laughed.

"Take the rope off him and I'll show you a new strain I think Buck may want to try with one or two of his mares next year," Williams suggested adding "and they are no kin to Max."

Kyle turned the colt loose, "lead the way," he replied, they walked over to a pasture that was fenced off and there were four mares and one stud plus, four-year-old colts, they weren't filled out quite like Max but, Kyle figured that was only because of no grain, he was impressed with their build. Kyle thought William has an eye for good horses, put these on a grain diet and they would be racers.

"What do you think," William asked.

"I think you have the right makings here," Kyle replied.

"I bought the stud and the mares from a young man who lost his dad over in Pennsylvania, the young man didn't want to farm, so he rented the land to a neighbor and he brought the horses by here and offered them to me for a very reasonable price and I bought them," William explained.

"People will fall in love with them," Kyle said, "they're beautifully built."

"That's what I thought to," William agreed, "I plan to mix the mares out of these with Maxes brother and see what I come up with."

"I'm thinking a runner," Kyle replied.

"Once again I think so too," William agreed, "perhaps Buck may be interested in one of these," He suggested."

"He probably will; if I know him," Kyle said, "I bet they will be stayers."

"I'm thinking they will be good horses for someone like soldiers," William said.

"Yeah for riding but, I don't think they're built right for pulling, they're what I call to stream lined, their muscles aren't bunched enough." Kyle said. "True; but they uses a lot of riding stock to," William pointed out. "Yes, and you mix these with Maxes brother I think it will add distance to their day," Max agreed.

"I think you're right," William agreed. "Well I think I'll let to spend some time with Lillie, only thing I ask from you is you treat here right; cause you know her mother will give her; her cast iron skillet," he teased.

"I have nothing but her best interests in mind," Kyle replied.

"I know that when you're tempted by another woman remember what could turn out, ten kids and over two hundred pounds," William reminded him.

"I think I understand," Kyle said, "be careful what you dream about because dreams can be cloudy," he suggested.

"Yes I think you do understand," William replied. They started back to the house by way of the barn, picking up Kyle and Lillie's horses as they walked up they found Lillie outside watching her brother and sister playing in the sandbox which William had made with the first of their children.

"You leaving already," Lillie asked.

"You can ride with him but, be back by dark," her dad said, "well Kyle when is the next time you're coming to see Lillie," he asked?

"It will probably be over a week," Kyle replied, "will probably be on Tuesday when I come to get the mare."

"That will be fine with me, but someone else may run away," William teased Lillie.

"You have no idea how much I want to go with him now," Lillie answered.

"Oh yes I do," Catherine replied, "I wanted to do the same thing with your dad but, he wouldn't let me, said not till were married," she added.

"I've heard the same thing," Lillie said, "I wish that preacher would come calling."

"He will not till we have our own homes and we get my mom and dad's blessing," Kyle assured her.

"Remind you of anyone," William asked?

"You were just like him and I'm glad," Catherine replied.

"Are you getting married Lillie," her little sister asked. Lillie nodded her head.

"Oh wow!" She cheered.

"That's how I feel to Catherine," her dad said. She giggled when her dad said that.

"Thank you for dinner and thanks comes from Buck for taking care of his mare and for having such a beautiful and wonderful daughter," Kyle said.

"You just mind what I said," William replied.

"I will," Kyle answered, "bye." Lillie was wondering what her dad had told Kyle, she'd ask him shortly, they mounted the horses and waved goodbye and headed toward the trail to the Valley.

"Your little sister summed up how I feel about marrying you." Kyle stated.

"Oh; now how's that," Lillie asked.

"Wow," Kyle replied.

"Me too," Lillie agreed, "what did you and my dad talk about," she asked?

"Iron skillet," Kyle answered, "and while some women may be tempting to me; the, ah later results may be heavy," he added.

"I guess that's good advice for me with men," she surmises.

"I think we should not allow ourselves to be tempted by someone else once we connect to someone so to speak, it only causes problems," Kyle said, "and besides having you how or why would I be tempted."
"I was thinking the same thing," Lillie replied.

"We know like with your mom and dad people look at others like your dad with Becky and my bosses wife won't let him come up here because the way he looks at your mother."

"Oh she won't," Lillie inquired.

"She said he can't think when your mother's around, says she's too beautiful," Kyle explain, "she is a good-looking woman herself and has nothing at all to worry about, and Buck will tell you he likes to look at beauty, it's one of his faults," he added.

"Don't you think it's normal," she asked?

"Yes I do," Kyle answered, "I think it's what you do after you look or if they are free or if one is and the other isn't, once that is known make the right choice."

"I agree," Lillie said.

"I can't think of anyone but you and don't want anyone else but you, so it works well," Kyle explained.

"When I wake up of a morning I think of you, where you are at, what are you doing and I think of you when I go to sleep, then I dream of you every night, I want to touch you and you're not there," Lillie explained.

"It the same for me," Kyle replied, "It's getting easier to work and think of you, the first few days I'd forget what I was doing, Buck would asked me if you were on my mine and laugh."

"It's good he don't get mad," Lillie said.

"He said he was the same way when he met his wife, once a limb took him off his horse, he was glad he'd ground reined trained his horse and it stopped, he was ten miles from anywhere and because of that he only uses split reins and has me trained all his horses to stand when they fall to the ground," Kyle explained, "he figures there will be others fall off their horse dreaming of love.

"That is probably true," Lillie said.

"Buck is more apt to laugh at someone than to get mad," Kyle said, "he says he doesn't like to get mad cause then he gets mad at his self for getting mad."

"I understand that if I get mad at something are someone, I usually ask myself why," Lillie said.

"If I got mad at horses every time they acted up I'd be mad a lot, and then I learned if you stay calm while working horses they are a lot calmer," Kyle explained.

"My dad needs to try that," Lillie said, "he does the brute strength way," she added.

"He saw a little different way I use today maybe he'll try it, and he's already asked me to see if Buck will let me teach your brothers how to train horses," Kyle said.

"Maybe," she replied, "What will I do when we marry," she asked?

"Well my mother cleaned some of the houses for some of the ranchers and wealthier people in town, she may need some help," Kyle suggested.

"I could do that," she acknowledged. They were at the pass to the Valley, "wow how did we get here so fast," she asked?

"Let's rest the horses," Kyle suggested, this suited Lillie fine; they tied their horses to a tree and went and sat on a log William had dragged into the shade for the purpose of setting on while resting the horses after the climb up the hill, first thing Lillie came into Kyle's arms and they kissed for a longer time, they came apart for just seconds came together kissing once more, finally Lillie backed off.

"I have to wait for other things but I don't want to," Lillie said. "We will be able to before you know it, real soon if Buck lets us rent one of his houses," Kyle assured her.

"Do you think he will," she asked?

"I think so," he replied, "I'll ask when I get home but, I'm sure he will."

"To feel you touch me every night and first thing of the morning, this will be a dream come true," Lillie change the subject.

"Yes and I dream the same about you and other things," Kyle confided. She laid her head upon his chess and stayed there for a while.

After of while Kyle said, "as much as I don't want to move we have to, your dad want you back by dark."

She sighed, "I know and kissed him again."

"Oh yes I can get used to this," Kyle stated.

"Me too," she replied, they untied their horses remounted and started down the trail to the valley below, once again they stopped to rest the horses.

"Want to check on my brothers while we're here," Lillie asked?

"Sure," Kyle answered, "lead the way." She led off across the valley toward what look like a solid tree line; part way down they found an opening that curved into a big field, Kyle thought maybe two hundred acres are more of grass and here and there were patches of cedar trees that had hay piled nearby.

"I would never have guessed there was this much open area here," Kyle said.

"The cedar trees that have hay by them have good springs by them," Lillie explained.

"If it snows a lot as it does some years the cows come here for food and shelter," Kyle finished for her.

"That's right," Lillie replied, she pointed, "there they are," and started towards them, they crossed by a place that was fenced it had alfalfa growing in it, Lillie pointed at it, "there are three patches of this here in the Valley."

Buck has ten acres of it, it keeps two men busy, plus Jim and I help put it in the loft," Kyle said. They rode over to where her brothers were cutting hay, now they were tossing hay in the wagon to stack, they cut hay of the morning and then stacked it in the afternoons if it was dry, if they got all that dry hay stack soon enough they would cut some more in the afternoon. Kyle noticed they had a lot of hay stacked.

"Dad's going to send y'all to Buck's," Lillie informed them.

"Your dad asked me to ask Buck if I could teach you two some of how I train horses for something like; breeding some of his mares to the new stud or Maxes line," Kyle explained.

"You must have impressed dad some for him to ask that," Bo stated.

"There may be more to you than we see," Ross said.

"Oh there is!" Lillie acknowledged.

"Well now we may not be blinded by what you are sis," Ross stated.

"You're just blind Ross, you think you have to do all by strength, he's figured out some things can be done by gentleness," Lillie explained, "and I can see with my eyes as well as my heart," she said.

"Well, well, you're tempers coming out." Ross taunted her.

"Not yet," Lillie replied adding, "you're still standing."

"If Buck agrees to this when would we do it," Bo asked?

"Late summer or early fall, your dad said," Kyle relayed.

"I figured," Ross said, "well we better get back to work."

"Okay I've got to be heading home soon anyway, I'll see you all later, bye," Kyle said. Lillie gave Ross the evil eye before she said, "goodbye," he laughed.

"Bye sis," Ross said. Bo just shook his head.

"Are you trying to get a black eye," Bo asked?

"No I'm just teasing sis," Ross replied. Lillie led as her and Kyle rode away.

"Now if dad wants us to watch or have Kyle to teach us about training horses, dad saw something," Ross surmised.

"Yeah you know and I know dads not easily impressed," Bo replied.

"True, Ross agreed, "we better get back to work, I like to get done before dark," he added.

"Does make one curious," Bo said, and they went back to loading hay.

Kyle and Lillie went across the field and through the opening, when she got to the other side she got off of her horse still mad at her brother."

"What's wrong," Kyle knew but ask anyway.

"My brother," she fumed,

Kyle took her into his arms and gently kissed her, "you know he's teasing you is all," he said softly as he eased some loose hair out of her face.

"I know," she replied. Kyle could physically feel the anger drain from her.

"I can take it from them don't worry," Kyle assured her, "does Ross have a girl he's sweet on," he asked?

"Not that I know of," she answered.

"Well when he does he'll think differently about a lot of things in his life," Kyle said, "I know I did."

"I see what you're saying and yes I look at things differently," Lillie replied. They kiss hungrily this time.

They came apart, "I hadn't wanted to leave you and couldn't wait to see you again the last time I was here and now it's time to go but, I want to go so I can get a home arranged to take you with me, if that makes any sense," Kyle asked?"

"Yes it does," Lillie replied they remount and slowly headed to Willows spring.

After a fast hour they parted with a long kiss, burning with desire, that and the thoughts of the all the things they needed for a home were on Kyle's mind as he headed home.

Lillie was thinking of caring for the home and Kyle, what would please him? How he like his food? Then she thought I cooked for him today and he liked it, she'd asked her mother, their minds were racing, Kyle was a long time getting home, thinking about the things that needed done, it was almost dark when he put his horse in the barn, Buck came outside and came to the barn as Kyle was coming out.

"I thought I heard you ride up," Buck said for a greeting.

"Yeah I just got in," Kyle acknowledged, "been an interesting day."

"Oh" Buck replied, you didn't get married while you were there, did you," he asked?

"No not yet," Kyle said.

"But you're going to," Buck finished for him.

"Can't keep anything from you can I," Kyle replied, "yes were going to and the sooner the better, and ah; do you have a house I can rent," he asked?

Buck chuckled and said, "For some reason I expected that question tonight, and yes I have two houses that you can live in," he answered. This answer was like a hundred pounds taken off of Kyle's shoulders.

"How much for the rent," Kyle asked?

"You keep winning races with my horses and there won't be any," Buck answered.

"Are you sure, that almost doesn't seem right," Kyle stated.

"Well I was going to give you a raise for the good job you're doing, so you can rent the house and will call ourselves even," Buck replied.

"Oh" if you're sure," Kyle asked?

"Completely sure," Buck assured him.

"Okay," Oh Lillie's dad asked me to ask you if this fall if he sent his two oldest sons here would you let me train them on training horses and how many stud fees would it cost him," Kyle asked?

"I'll have to think about that, we'll have an answer before you go back up there,"

Buck explained.

"He also told me to think about some of the mares you have that might go good with another string of horses he bought from a rancher from Pennsylvania," Kyle informed him.

"What did you think of them," Buck asked.

"My first impression of the stud and the mares was they were stayers for the long haul, and William and I were thinking on the same lines he had thought about offering them to the Army, the Colts that is, for re-mounts," Kyle replied. "And I thought that some of these colt's that are not quite up to the top-of-the-line mixed with these might boost them up," he added.

"Does he have colts out of these," he asked?

"Yes they are about one-year-olds," Kyle answered.

"Interesting, we may have to see if he will turn loose of one of the young studs," Buck said, "now I wasn't expecting either one of the last two questions today, so when are you planning on getting married," he asked?

"Well soon and if I would have let her she would've came home with me today," Kyle answered.

"So like next weekend," Buck asks?

"Maybe I didn't specify to her," he replied adding, "I have her parents blessing, her dad said without it she would just run off anyway."

"Well I knew this morning when you left the deal was signed, sealed and all was left was a preacher," Buck chuckled."

"That's one way to put it, I am excited and scared at same time," Kyle omitted.

"Scared of what," Buck asked?

"Well I'm not real up to date on women," Kyle explained.

Buck got a good laugh I out of this, "boy do I know how you feel, I was the same way when I got married, and I can tell you don't worry about it we have a natural built-in knowledge that will take care of it," Buck assured him.

"Oh! "really," Kyle asked?

"Yes, really" Buck replied, "don't you have a something to go ask for from your parents," he asked?

Yes I do and mom is probably keeping me something to eat so I better go," Kyle replied. Buck chuckled at the expression on Kyle's face that of concern.

"Kyle, we are no different than animals on this farm, y'all will figure it out with no problem," Buck explained, and watched the light come on Kyle's expression.

"OH!" Now I understand," Kyle replied. "Well good night Buck and thank you, I will see you in the morning," he said as he started walking home.

"Good night Kyle," Buck replied, he turned and was chuckling when he went in the house.

"What are you chuckling about," Beth asked.

"Oh were going to have a marriage in the neighborhood very soon," Buck replied.

"Really, Kyle," Sarah inquired?

"Yes and Williams daughter, I think he said her name is Lillie," Buck answered.

"Well that is good, perhaps he'll forget about running off to the wild blue yonder," she stated.

"With our conversation we had this morning, I think he's forgot that already, and I'd say after they figure things out that desire will vanish," Buck predicted.

"Oh I see he's worried about that," Beth stated and chuckled, they'll be fine.

"I agree," Buck said.

Shortly Kyle made it home and Peter was standing at the door looking out for him, he heard him say "here comes Kyle but she's not with him," he stated sadly. Kyle thought to his self she is with me more than you know little brother.

"You didn't think he was gone to bring her home today did you," Katie asked.

"Why yes he's going to marry her," Peter announced. Once again Kyle thought his little brother was very wise to know what was going to occur before it does, funny how a child's mind works.

"It doesn't happen quite that fast," Barnabas explained.

"It does this time," Peter insisted, "they're getting married."

"We'll ask him when he comes in," Katie replied.

"You'll ask me what," Kyle asked from the door?

"Peter has the notion you were getting married today," Katie asked.

"Well not today Peter, but he is right with your permission very soon," Kyle replied.

"Oh," Katie responded.

"How soon is soon," Barnabas asked?

"Well I have a house already," Kyle said, "next week."

"Maybe its best," Katie said.

"Her dad's reply was she is like her mother and if they said no she would run away," Kyle explained.

"You think you should take some time to think about it," Barnabas asked.

"Her dad said that also and we went for a three-hour ride looking at their livestock," Kyle said, "and probably yes but the thinking part is all we think about so we plan to marry," he stated.

"But; come on in the kitchen I saved you some supper," Katie said.

"Thank you," Kyle said, as he made his way to the kitchen.

Peter followed him into the kitchen, "will you be moving to her house," Peter asked.

"No," Kyle answered, "we'll be moving just down the road," he added.

"That's good didn't want you to be too far away," he replied.

"I'm not trying to talk you out of getting married I just guess I want you to be sure," Barnabas stated.

"I understand and I don't normally make snap decisions like this," Kyle said, "you see I've have never been more sure of anything in my life."

"Your mother and I married like you did, in a hurry and I don't know why I'm worried because we had no regrets for that decision," Barnabas said, "so yes you have our blessings," he added. Peter ran into the other room and announced, "Kyle's getting married." His sisters cheered, Kyle was smiling from ear to ear as he sat down and started eating supper.

"You have a lot of things you're going to need," Katie said.

"They're going to have to cut wood, both for cooking now and heating this winter," Barnabas said, "there is a big holler behind one of the house of Bucks and we've got some I may be able to get near the mine, that would help you out a lot."

"Yes and you should plant some of the shorter seasons vegetables in a garden are its going to be too late," Katie added.

"Fortunately both of the houses are in good shape now I won't have to work on the one we move in," Kyle said.

"Well you know you always had to do some work on the house it's called up keep," Barnabas corrected him.

"Yeah I know that," Kyle acknowledged "what I meant by that was he had both painted and the roofs worked on earlier this year."

"That's a good start," Barnabas said, "what about the wells," he asked?

"They share one," he answered.

"It sounds like they are in good shape then," Katie put in, "have you thought about things your wife might need," she asked?

"I thought about that on the way home and had hoped maybe you and Lillie's mother could go help her get what is needed for the house and her, at my expense a course," Kyle explained.

"I'm sure we can arrange something," she answered, "sometime next week if you can get Buck to let Robert, borrow a horse he can go up and ask, "What is her name," she asked?

"Catherine, the same as yours" Kyle answered.

"Okay, ask her if she would meet me in town with Lillie of course and get some of the things she'll need," Katie replied.

"I will ask Buck," Kyle said, "and I'm sure he will."

"Do you know of any furniture or perhaps a cook stove," Barnabas asked?

"I believe there's a cook stove in both," Kyle said.

"They both have a table and chairs, cabinets and wash basins," Jim added.

"Is there any other furniture in them," Katie asked him?

"None that I recall," Jim replied.

"That's a pretty good start," Katie said, "a lot more than we had."

"That is true," Barnabas said, we had are clothing and what money we had which wasn't much," he added.

"Don't you think that made it easier for us," Katie asked?

"It made it easier to decide to come to America," Barnabas responded, "but we had much more,"

"Oh," Katie asked?

"Each other," Barnabas responded.

"Well yeah, there was that and for a little while that was what we lived on," Katie added. By this time in the conversation Kyle was through eating and got up an went into his room and got some clean clothes.

"There's still plenty of water in the kettle if you want to take a bath," Barnabas Jr said.

"Oh good that will beat a sponge bath," Kyle replied, "we'll talk more this week about what is needed and the marriage in general, he went outside and put water in the bath tub and got undress took his bath.

By the time he got inside most everyone was in bed his mother was in the kitchen she was the only one up.

"I'm very happy for you Kyle," his mother said.

"Thank you," Kyle replied, "you think this is the right thing and will be best for my future."

"We have to choose our own path but yes, this is a good one," Katie replied.

"Good night," Kyle said, and went to his bedroom, Barnabas was already asleep, and Jim set up when he walked in.

"A big day huh," Jim asked?

"Yes it was," Kyle replied, "it will add a lot of responsibility and yet it took a load off my mind, wondering if I should get married or not and now I'm very happy with the decision."

"Well I'm happy for you brother, good night," Jim said as he lay down."

"Good night," Kyle replied and lay down, and he like Lillie wrestled with their future before giving in to sleep and then dreamed of their kiss and what was to come.

CPSIA information can be obtained
at www.ICGtesting.com
Printed in the USA
BVHW072347220221
600780BV00008B/873